'This Glossary is impressively exhaustive in its coverage. It will be an indispensable aid to students in linguistics and other disciplines who need to understand a theory which is now coming of age, and advanced researchers will also find it a useful companion both for reference and for helping to access original texts.'

Professor Chris Sinha, University of Portsmouth

'Cognitive Linguistics is now developing rapidly, and, like all new fields, this one has developed its own technical meta-language. Anyone needing a jargon-free guide through this fascinating new terrain will find exactly what is needed in Vyv Evans' joined-up explanations of the landmark concepts and theories. The Glossary is far more than an alphabetical list – it gives unity and coherence to the Cognitive Linguistics project.'

Professor Paul Chilton, University of Lancaster

D1423638

A Glossary of Cognitive Linguistics

Vyvyan Evans

Edinburgh University Press

This book is dedicated to Max and Isabella

© Vyvyan Evans, 2007

Edinburgh University Press Ltd
22 George Square, Edinburgh

Typeset in Sabon
by Servis Filmsetting Ltd, Manchester, and
printed and bound in Great Britain by
Antony Rowe Ltd, Chippenham, Wilts

A CIP record for this book is available from the British Library

ISBN 978 0 7486 2279 5 (hardback)
ISBN 978 0 7486 2280 1 (paperback)

Contents

Preface

About cognitive linguistics

Cognitive linguistics is a modern school of linguistic thought that originally emerged in the early 1970s. It is also firmly rooted in the emergence of modern cognitive science in the 1960s and 1970s, particularly in work relating to human categorisation, and in earlier traditions such as Gestalt psychology. Cognitive linguistics is primarily concerned with investigating the relationship between language, the mind and socio-physical experience. The earliest pioneers in cognitive linguistics were responding, in part, to dissatisfaction with formal approaches to language. Early research, especially in the 1970s, was dominated by a relatively small group of scholars based on the western seaboard of the United States. During the 1980s, cognitive linguistic research began to take root in northern continental Europe, particularly in Belgium, Holland and Germany. By the early 1990s, there was a growing proliferation of research in cognitive linguistics throughout Europe and North America, and a relatively large internationally distributed group of researchers who identified themselves as 'cognitive linguists'. In 1989/1990, the International Cognitive Linguistics Society was established, together with the journal *Cognitive Linguistics*. In the words of Ronald Langacker ([1991] 2002: xv), this 'marked the birth of cognitive linguistics as a broadly grounded, self conscious intellectual movement.' Today, cognitive linguistics is one of the most rapidly expanding schools of theoretical linguistics with a flourishing international cognitive linguistics community and national cognitive linguistics associations in many countries throughout the world. Due to its interdisciplinary nature, it is also one of the most exciting areas of study within cognitive science.

Further details about cognitive linguistics, including its historical development, its founding principles and assumptions, and some of the main theoretical approaches which populate it, are provided in an article length overview: see Evans, Bergen and Zinken (2007). For a comprehensive book-length introduction see Evans and Green (2006).

About this Glossary

This Glossary represents an introduction to the hitherto two best developed areas of cognitive linguistics: cognitive semantics and cognitive approaches to grammar. That is, this Glossary represents an introduction to terms that have a special status in cognitive linguistics. Hence, it is not a Glossary of terms in general linguistics nor in cognitive science. Accordingly, it does not include entries for terms that have currency outside cognitive linguistics, unless such terms have a 'special' status or interpretation within cognitive linguistics.

One of the difficulties in compiling a book of this sort lies in the fact that cognitive linguistics (and its two significant sub-branches) represents an *approach* to the study of language, the mind and embodied experience, rather than a single closely articulated *theory*. The consequence of this is that now, after nearly three decades since the publication of Lakoff and Johnson's *Metaphors We Live By* in 1980, there is a wide range of distinctive theoretical frameworks which are cognitive linguistic in nature, and which each have their own specialist terms and vocabulary.

To be sure, there are many terms employed in cognitive linguistics that enjoy wide currency within the field. Nevertheless, there are many others which are primarily used within the context of one of the two main sub-branches. There are also other terms that are only used in the context of a specific approach or theory. Hence there are inherent difficulties in selecting the terms to be covered so as to avoid a volume of this sort becoming too unwieldy.

In order to constrain the nature and scope of terms covered in this volume, the selection has been based on the terms used in *Cognitive Linguistics: An Introduction*, authored by Vyvyan Evans and Melanie Green. For the most part I have selected from the terms used in that book as the basis for this volume, with a few additions. This has necessarily meant that some relatively important terms are not covered in this volume. However, this would have been the case even with a volume twice the size of the present one. The rationale behind selecting terms based on the Evans and Green book is that the present volume, while it could indeed be used as a stand-alone work of reference, can also be employed by instructors and students as a companion volume to the Evans and Green textbook. This, I hope, will bring with it more advantages than disadvantages, not least in that it provides a handy listing in A–Z format of many of the key terms featured in the Evans and Green textbook.

The entries provided in this Glossary have been written in a way so that related terms from within the same theory can be read in conjunction with one another, providing a useable characterisation of a related and overlapping set of ideas rather than merely providing 'dictionary-like' definitions. Entries contain items in bold-face, which lead to further entries. By following items in bold-face through the Glossary, it is envisaged that the reader should be able to get a basic grasp of the key theories, approaches, principles and other ideas in cognitive linguistics and some of the key theoretical constructs within each of the theories and approaches covered. The reader can then refer to the Evans and Green textbook introduction for more detailed explication and examples.

Alternatively, the interested reader can use the Glossary as a means of delving deeper into the by now voluminous literature in cognitive linguistics. In order to aid this process, the Glossary features an annotated list of further reading at the end of the book. This includes textbooks, works of reference and essential 'primary literature' addressing all the areas of cognitive linguistics covered in the Glossary. In addition, key researchers associated with each of the constructs and/or theories are identified. The first mention of a key researcher in cognitive linguistics in each entry is italicised. There is a listing of all such named scholars at the end of the Glossary, together with keywords relating to the areas of investigation with which they are associated. It is envisaged that this listing can be used as a means of further identifying and narrowing topics and scholars of interest for further reading.

Cognitive linguistics offers exciting glimpses into hitherto hidden aspects of the human mind, human experience and, by consequence, what it is to be human. I hope that by making the technical language associated with cognitive linguistics more readily accessible, students, interested lay-readers and scholars from neighbouring disciplines may thus be able to get a glimpse into what it is that makes those of us engaged in cognitive linguistics research so excited.

Vyvyan Evans
Brighton, September 2006
www.vyvevans.net

References

Evans, Vyvyan and Melanie Green (2006) *Cognitive Linguistics: An Introduction*. Mahwah, NJ and Edinburgh: Edinburgh University Press/Lawrence Erlbaum Associates.

Evans, Vyvyan, Benjamin Bergen and Jörg Zinken (2007) 'The Cognitive Linguistics Enterprise: An Overview', in V. Evans, B. Bergen and J. Zinken (eds), *The Cognitive Linguistics Reader*. London: Equinox.

Lakoff, George and Mark Johnson (1980) *Metaphors We Live By*. Chicago: University of Chicago Press.

Langacker, Ronald ([1991] 2002) *Concept, Image, Symbol*, 2nd edn. Berlin: Mouton de Gruyter.

abstract domain A **domain (1)** which is not directly
grounded in **embodied experience** and thus stands in
contrast to a **basic domain**. Abstract domains include
MARRIAGE, LOVE or MEDIEVAL MUSICOLOGY. Although
such domains are ultimately derived from embodied
experience, they are more complex in nature. For
instance, our knowledge of LOVE may involve knowledge relating to basic domains, such as directly embodied experiences like touch, sexual relations and
physical proximity, and may also involve knowledge
relating to abstract domains, such as experience of
complex social activities like marriage ceremonies,
hosting dinner parties and so on. (See also **Cognitive
Grammar.**)

abstraction (1) In a **usage-based model** of language, the
process whereby structure emerges as the result of
the generalisation of patterns across instances of language use. For example, a speaker acquiring English
will, as the result of frequent exposure, 'discover'
recurring words, phrases and sentences in the utterances they hear, together with the range of meanings
associated with those units. A special kind of abstraction is **schematisation**. (See also **usage-based thesis,
utterance.**)

abstraction (2) One of the three **parameters of focal adjustment**. Relates to how specific or detailed the description of a scene is. This also has consequences for the type of construction selected. Consider the following examples:

1. Isabella threw a rattle at the TV and smashed it
2. Isabella smashed the TV

The example in (2) is more abstract (less detailed) than the example in (1). In this way, abstraction relates to the level of attention paid to a scene, in terms of level of detail. (See also **construal, focal adjustment, perspective, selection**.)

access Refers to the phenomenon in **LCCM Theory** whereby the selection of a given **lexical concept** makes a particular **cognitive model profile** accessible for **activation**. In practice only a small part of a cognitive model profile is ever activated in the construction of any given **conception**. (See also **access site, cognitive model, lexical concept selection**.)

Access Principle (also **ID Principle**) Captures one of the central structuring properties associated with **mental space** formation and their proliferation in terms of a **mental spaces lattice**. The Access Principle holds that any linguistic expression that names or describes a particular element in a given mental space may be employed in order to access an element in a distinct mental space that is linked to it via a connector. In other words, the Access Principle captures the insight that an element in one mental space can be accessed by its counterpart element in another by virtue of the **counterparts** being related by **connectors**.

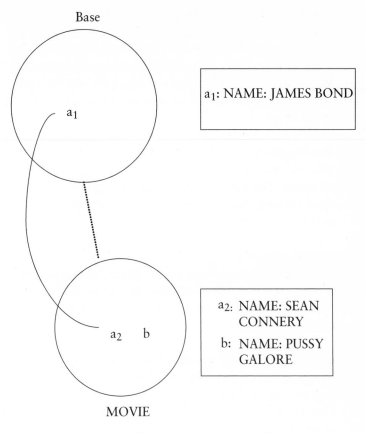

Figure 1. Illustration of the Access Principle

To illustrate, consider the following example: *James Bond is a top British spy. In the film, Sean Connery gets to kiss Pussy Galore*. In this example, each sentence sets up its own mental space, involving the elements *James Bond* in the first, and *Sean Connery* and *Pussy Galore* in the second. As James Bond and Sean Connery (the actor who played James Bond in the movie *Goldfinger*) are counterparts linked by a connector, the expression

Sean Connery can be used to access or identify the character he plays: we are meant to understand that in the movie it is James Bond (rather than Sean Connery who is not in fact a spy) who does the kissing. This is set in diagrammatic form in Figure 1 where the circles represent distinct mental spaces and the elements in each, James Bond (a_1) and Sean Connery (a_2) are linked by a connector, signalled by the line relating a_1 and a_2. (See also **Mental Spaces Theory, Optimisation Principle**.)

access route The path of **activation** through a **cognitive model profile** afforded by a **lexical concept** given the particular linguistic and extralinguistic context in which it is embedded. (See also **access, access site, LCCM Theory**.)

access site The point in a **cognitive model profile** where a **lexical concept** affords **access**. (See also **access route, LCCM Theory**.)

action chain A model proposed in **Cognitive Grammar** which serves as the conceptual basis for the semantic notions of AGENT and PATIENT. An action chain involves an active 'energy source' that transfers energy to an 'energy sink'. The 'prototypical action' is characterised in terms of the transfer of energy from AGENT to PATIENT, resulting in a change of state of the PATIENT, as in the following sentence: *Isabella smashed the TV*. This is illustrated in Figure 2, where A represents AGENT and P represents PATIENT.

activation The process, in **LCCM Theory**, whereby part of the **semantic potential** to which a **lexical concept** affords **access** is recruited for purposes of local communication in a given **utterance**.

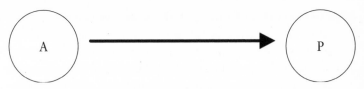

Figure 2. The prototypical action chain model

active zone That part of an entity which is cognitively activated, and thus 'active', by virtue of linguistic context. For instance, in examples such as the following:

1. Max heard the trumpet
2. Max saw the trumpet

the verbs *hear* and *saw* serve to activate different aspects of our knowledge associated with trumpets. In (1), the active zone relates to knowledge concerning the kind of sound emitted by trumpets, while in (2) the active zone concerns the visual properties associated with trumpets, such as their shape and colour. The notion of an active zone is an important construct in **Cognitive Grammar.**

altered replication The process of language change whereby **innovation** occurs. Altered replication takes place when a **replicator** is altered slightly in an **utterance.** For an innovation to give rise to language change, the **lingueme** which has been subject to altered replication must undergo **propagation** through a language community. Altered replication can involve both an innovation with respect to form, for instance the sound pattern of a given word, or use, for example the meaning associated with a given word. (See also **usage-based thesis, Utterance Selection Theory.**)

argument roles In **Construction Grammar (2)**, a semantic 'slot' associated with sentence-level constructions such as **verb argument constructions**. Argument roles include AGENT and PATIENT and contrast with the more specific construct of **participant roles**. (See also **constructional profiling, fusion (1)**.)

argument structure (also **valence**) The number of arguments, that is participants or entities, that a word-level **relational predication** such as a verb may be combined with. For instance, a verb like *die* only involves a single participant: *She died*, while a verb such as *love* involves two: *I love you*, and a verb like *put* involves three: *He put the butter on the table*. The notion of argument structure is central to the **verb argument constructions** studied in **Construction Grammar (2)**.

Atemporal relations A sub-category of the larger category **relational predication**. Atemporal relations include prepositions, adjectives, adverbs and non-finite verb forms (infinitives and participles), and contrast with **temporal relations**. The domain of TIME underlies the distinction between temporal and atemporal relations. Atemporal relations are accessed via **summary scanning**. Atemporal relations can be divided into two types: **simple atemporal relations** and **complex atemporal relations**. (See also **conceived time, processing time, sequential scanning**.)

attentional system One of the four **schematic systems** which form part of the **conceptual structuring system**. The attentional system governs the distribution of attention over matter and action (scenes and their participants), and is governed by three main factors: **strength, pattern**, and **mapping**. (See also **Conceptual**

Structuring System Approach, configurational system, force-dynamics system, perspectival system, schematic categories.)

autonomy A termed coined by *Alan Cruse* in his approach to lexical semantics. Refers to the degree of conventionalisation associated with a word-meaning that secures relative context-independence and thus identifies a distinct sense. Examples of word senses which are not fully autonomous include a **sub-sense** and a **facet**.

axiality One of the **schematic categories** in the **configurational system**. Axiality relates to the way a quantity of SPACE or TIME is structured according to a directed axis. For example, the adjectives *well* and *sick* are points on an axis relating to HEALTH. On the axis, *well* is the endpoint, whereas *sick* is the remainder of the axis. This explains the different distribution of the closed class degree modifiers like *almost* and *slightly*. While it is possible to be *slightly sick* or *almost well*, it is not possible to be **slightly well* or **almost sick*. This follows from the axiality model because it is not possible to be 'slightly' at an endpoint, nor 'almost' on the journey towards that endpoint. This is illustrated in Figure 3. (See also **boundedness**, **Conceptual Structuring System Approach**, **degree of extension**, **dividedness**, **pattern of distribution**, **plexity**, **schematic systems**.)

axial properties In a **spatial scene** the figure is located by virtue of the axial properties associated with a given **reference object**. For instance, in a sentence of the following kind: *The bike is in front of the house*, *the bike* can be located by virtue of 'searching' for the bike, the figure, in the **region** in front of the house. However,

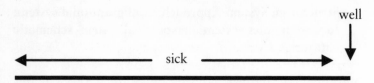

Figure 3. The axiality model

this process occurs by virtue of the reference object, *the house*, having a number of 'axial' divisions: front, back and side areas. These areas of the reference object constitute axial properties and are employed in the establishment of a **spatial relation**. Some reference objects are symmetric and thus fail to manifest intrinsic axial properties. In such situations a **secondary reference object** is required in order to provide the (primary) reference object with axial properties. (See also **reference frame, figure-ground organisation**.)

Aymara An indigenous language of South America, spoken in the Andean region of Peru, Chile and Bolivia. Aymara is notable for the way in which it structures time. *Rafael Núñez* and *Eve Sweetser* report that while Aymara features variants of both an **ego-based cognitive model for time** and a **time-based cognitive model for time**, in the ego-based model, Aymara speakers conceptualise the FUTURE as being located behind the ego, while PAST is conceptualised as being in front of the ego. (See also **cognitive models for time, moving ego model, moving time model**.)

B

backstage cognition A term coined by *Gilles Fauconnier*. Refers to the observation that much of what goes on in the construction of meaning occurs 'behind the scenes'. Fauconnier argues that language does not encode thought in its complex entirety but encodes rudimentary instructions for the creation of rich and elaborate ideas. Fauconnier gives the label 'backstage cognition' to these 'behind-the-scenes' **conceptualisation** processes that are involved in meaning construction.

backward projection A consequence of **conceptual integration**. As the **input spaces** in an **integration network** remain connected to the **blended space,** they can be modified as a result of emergent structure in the blended space: the process of backward projection. For instance, consider the CLINTON AS FRENCH PRESIDENT blend discussed in the entry for conceptual integration, and which arises due to the following utterance: *In France, Clinton would not have been harmed by his affair Monica Lewinsky.* The structure that emerges in the blended space is projected back to the input spaces. This is the process that gives rise to the disanalogy between the USA and France. In other words, a contrast is established between the nature of French and American moral attitudes governing the behaviour of politicians. (See also **Blending Theory.**)

base That part of the **domain matrix** necessary for understanding the **profile** of a **linguistic unit**. For instance, the lexical item *hypotenuse* profiles the longest side of a right-angled triangle. The base constitutes the larger structure, the right-angled triangle, of which the hypotenuse constitutes a sub-structure. The larger structure, the base, is essential for understanding the notion **hypotenuse**. (See also **Cognitive Grammar, scope of predication.**)

base space The **mental space** which represents the starting point for a particular stage in discourse, such as the beginning of a conversation. The base space serves to set up the discourse; it is with respect to the base space that a **mental spaces lattice** is anchored. In ongoing discourse, the base space is the mental space to which the conversation can return at any time. (See also **event space, focus space, Mental Spaces Theory, viewpoint space**.)

basic domain A **domain** (1) which derives directly from human **embodied experience**, and which stands in contrast to an **abstract domain**. Basic domains are derived from both **sensory experience** and **subjective experience**. A non-exhaustive list of basic domains, and their experiential basis, is given in Table 1. (See also **Cognitive Grammar**.)

basic level According to **Prototype Theory**, the level of category formation which is held to be optimal for human beings in terms of **cognitive economy**. This level of categorisation provides a level of information at the mid-level of detail, between the most inclusive and least inclusive levels: the superordinate and the subordinate levels respectively. The basic level is associated with categories like CAR, DOG and CHAIR. The superordinate level (more inclusive) is associated with categories such as vehicle, animal and furniture. The subordinate level (less inclusive) is associated with categories such as SPORTSCAR, COLLIE and ROCKING CHAIR, respectively. The basic level also maximises differences between categories at the same level. For instance, a CAR is extremely distinct from a DOG (both are at the basic level), whereas a COLLIE is relatively less distinct from an ALSATIAN (both at the subordinate

Table 1. Basic domains

Basic domain	Pre-conceptual basis
SPACE	Visual system; motion and position (proprioceptive) sensors in skin, muscles and joints; vestibular system (located in the auditory canal; detects motion and balance)
COLOUR	Visual system
PITCH	Auditory system
TEMPERATURE	Tactile (touch) system
PRESSURE	Pressure sensors in the skin, muscles and joints
PAIN	Detection of tissue damage by nerves under the skin
ODOUR	Olfactory (smell) system
TIME	Temporal awareness
EMOTION	Affective (emotion) system

level). It has been claimed by *Eleanor Rosch* that categories formed at the basic level tend to emerge first both developmentally and in language acquisition, and categories at this level are most easily recognised and identified. (See also **cue validity, prototype, prototype structure.**)

blend see **blended space**

blended space (also **blend**) In an **integration network,** the **mental space** which results from **conceptual integration,** giving rise to **emergent structure.** (See also **Blending Theory.**)

blending see **conceptual integration**

Blending Theory (also known as **Conceptual Blending Theory, Conceptual Integration Theory, Many Space Model**) Developed by *Gilles Fauconnier and Mark Turner*, Blending Theory derives from two traditions within **cognitive semantics: Conceptual Metaphor Theory** and **Mental Spaces Theory**. Blending Theory holds that meaning construction involves integration of structure that gives rise to more than the sum of its parts. The mechanism that facilitates this, known as **conceptual integration** or 'blending', is held to be a general and basic cognitive operation which is central to the way we think. In terms of its architecture, and in terms of its central concerns, Blending Theory is most closely related to Mental Spaces Theory, not least due to its use of mental spaces and **mental space** construction as a key part of its architecture. However, Blending Theory is a distinct theory that has been developed to account for phenomena that Mental Spaces Theory, and indeed Conceptual Metaphor Theory, cannot adequately account for. Moreover, Blending Theory adds significant theoretical sophistication of its own.

Blending Theory was originally developed in order to account for the role of language in meaning construction, particularly 'creative' aspects of meaning construction like novel metaphors, counterfactuals and so on. However, recent research has given rise to the view that conceptual blending is central to human thought and imagination, and that evidence for this can be found not only in human language, but also in a wide range of other areas of human activity. In particular, Fauconnier and Turner argue that the ability to perform conceptual integration or blending may have been the key mechanism in facilitating the development of advanced human behaviours that rely on complex symbolic abilities. These include rituals, art, tool manufacture and use, and the development of language. (See also **constitutive processes, goals of blending, governing principles, integration network**.)

bodily mimesis see **mimesis**

boundedness One of the **schematic categories** in the **configurational system**. Boundedness relates to whether a quantity is understood as having inherent boundaries (bounded) or not (unbounded). In the domain of SPACE, this is the basis of the count/mass noun distinction. For example, count nouns like *nightdress* and *blouse* have bounded structure, in that each designates an entity with inherent 'edges', which can thus be individuated and counted. On the other hand, mass nouns like *champagne* and *money* do not have inherent 'edges' and therefore cannot be individuated and counted. In the domain of TIME, boundedness is the basis of the distinction between perfect and imperfect grammatical aspect, as illustrated below:

1. Max has left the toy shop   [Perfect]
2. Max is leaving the toy shop   [Imperfect]

Example (1) is grammatically marked for perfect aspect by the presence of the perfect auxiliary *have* followed by the past participle *left*. Perfect aspect encodes an event that is completed and can thus be thought of as bounded. Example (2) is grammatically marked for imperfect (progressive) aspect by the progressive auxiliary *be*, followed by the progressive participle *leaving*. Imperfect aspect encodes an event that is 'ongoing' and can thus be thought of as unbounded. (See also **Conceptual Structuring System Approach, degree of extension, dividedness, pattern of distribution, plexity, schematic systems**.)

building block metaphor A term coined by *Ronald Langacker*. Relates to the view, held by scholars in **formal linguistics**, that the meaning of a complex expression is the result of compositionally adding the meaning of the individual units, the 'principle of compositionality'. For Langacker, and others in **cognitive linguistics**, this principle is erroneous.

C

caused motion construction One of the **verb argument constructions** studied by *Adele Goldberg* in the development of her theory of **Construction Grammar (2)**. This **construction (1)** has the syntax [SUBJ [V OBJ OBL]], where OBL (which is short for 'oblique' object) denotes a directional PP. The construction has the semantics X CAUSES Y TO MOVE Z, where Z designates a path of motion expressed by the directional PP. The construction is illustrated by the following example: *Max sneezed the birthday cards off the table*. Like several of the constructions studied by Goldberg, the caused motion construction exhibits **constructional polysemy**. The properties of the construction are summarised in Table 2. (See also **argument roles**.)

Table 2. Properties of the English caused motion construction

The English caused-motion construction: X CAUSES Y TO MOVE Z
Contributes CAUSED MOTION semantics that cannot be attributed to the lexical verb
Contributes CAUSED MOTION semantics that cannot be attributed to the preposition
The CAUSER argument role cannot be an INSTRUMENT

chaining A phenomenon exhibited in a **radial category** between distinct senses (or **lexical concepts**) associated with a given word. Chaining relates to the situation whereby new senses emerge that are intermediate with respect to the **prototype** (or **ideal meaning**) and the peripheral senses. Chaining is therefore the phenomenon whereby the central and peripheral senses are connected by virtue of intermediate senses. The range of mechanisms that have been proposed within the **cognitive lexical semantics** literature as giving rise to chaining include **metaphor, metonymy, image schema transformation** and **pragmatic strengthening**.

classical category A category, so called because it is possible to provide necessary and jointly sufficient conditions for determining that an entity belongs to a particular category. Examples of such categories include the categories BACHELOR and ODD NUMBER. Nevertheless, since the advent of *Eleanor Rosch's* work on **Prototype Theory** it has become clear that even classical categories exhibit **typicality effects**. For instance, some members of the ODD NUMBER category such as 1, 3, 5 and 9 are typically judged as being better examples of the category than high odd numbers such as 1001. (See also **Classical Theory**.)

Classical Theory The widely accepted account of the way humans categorise that was the prevalent model from the time of Aristotle until the early 1970s. This theory holds that conceptual and linguistic categories have 'definitional structure'. This means that an entity represents a category member by virtue of fulfilling a set of necessary and (jointly) sufficient conditions for category membership. These conditions are called 'necessary and sufficient' because they are individually necessary but only collectively sufficient to define a category. Traditionally, the conditions were thought to be sensory or perceptual in nature. To illustrate, consider the category BACHELOR. For an entity to belong to this category, it must adhere to the following conditions: 'is not married'; 'is male'; 'is an adult'. Each of these conditions is necessary for defining the category, but none of them is individually sufficient, because 'is not married' could equally hold for SPINSTER, while 'is male' could equally hold for HUSBAND, and so on. During the 1970s experimental findings which emerged under the banner of **Prototype Theory** showed the Classical Theory of categorisation to be implausible as a model of human categorisation.

closed class forms A set of linguistic forms to which it is typically more difficult for a language to add new members. Closed class forms are normally taken to include the 'grammatical' or 'function' words of a language. In English these include articles, prepositions, pronouns, inflectional morphemes and so forth. In terms of the meaning contributed by the closed class elements they provide **schematic meaning**. They contribute to the interpretation of an **utterance** in important but often subtle ways, providing a kind of 'scaffolding' which supports and structures the **content meaning** provided by **open class forms**. (See also **conceptual structuring system, implicit closed class form, overt closed class form**.)

cluster model Consists of a number of converging **ICMs** which collectively give rise to a complex cluster which thus forms a stable large-scale model. The cluster model is held to be psychologically more complex than the individual ICMs which comprise it. According to

George Lakoff who developed the notion of ICMs, the category MOTHER is an instance of cluster model. Lakoff suggests that the MOTHER cluster model is made up of the following ICMs:

1. THE BIRTH MODEL: a mother is the person who gives birth to the child.
2. THE GENETIC MODEL: a mother is the person who provides the genetic material for the child.
3. THE NURTURANCE MODEL: a mother is the person who brings up and looks after the child.
4. THE MARITAL MODEL: a mother is married to the child's father.
5. THE GENEALOGICAL MODEL: a mother is a particular female ancestor.

coding In **Cognitive Grammar**, the process whereby a speaker searches for a linguistic expression in order to express a **concept**. If the **symbolic assembly** the speaker arrives at matches symbolic assemblies existing in his or her inventory, this represents a case of **sanction** and thus well-formedness.

cognition Relates to all aspects of conscious and unconscious mental function. In particular, cognition constitutes the mental events (mechanisms and processes) and knowledge involved in a whole host of tasks ranging from 'low-level' object **perception** to 'high-level' decision-making tasks.

cognitive approaches to grammar A cognitive approach to grammar is concerned with modelling the language system (the mental 'grammar') in ways which are consistent with the **generalisation commitment** and the **cognitive commitment** associated with the larger **cognitive**

linguistics enterprise. Cognitive approaches also adhere to the two **guiding principles of cognitive approaches to grammar**. These are the **symbolic thesis** and the **usage-based thesis**. In addition, cognitive approaches take as their starting point the conclusions of work in **cognitive semantics**. This follows as meaning is central to cognitive approaches to grammar; although the study of cognitive semantics and cognitive approaches to grammar are occasionally separate in practice, this by no means implies that their domains of enquiry are anything but tightly linked. Indeed, most work in cognitive linguistics finds it necessary to investigate both semantics and grammar in tandem.

Researchers who adopt a cognitive approach to grammar have typically adopted one of two foci. Scholars such as *Ronald Langacker* have emphasised the study of the cognitive principles that give rise to linguistic organisation. In his theory of **Cognitive Grammar**, Langacker has attempted to delineate the principles that structure a grammar and to relate these to aspects of general cognition.

The second avenue of investigation, pursued by researchers including *William Croft*, *Charles Fillmore* and *Paul Kay*, *Adele Goldberg*, *George Lakoff*, *Laura Michaelis* and others, and more recently *Benjamin Bergen and Nancy Chang*, aims to provide a more descriptively and formally detailed account of the linguistic units that comprise a particular language. These researchers attempt to provide a broad-ranging inventory of the units of language, from morphemes to words, **idiomatic expressions** and phrasal patterns, and seek accounts of their structure, compositional possibilities and relations. Researchers who have pursued this line of investigation are developing a set of theories that are collectively known as **construction**

grammars. This general approach takes its name from the view in cognitive linguistics that the basic unit of language is a form-meaning pairing known as a **construction (1)**. (See also **linguistic unit**.)

cognitive commitment One of the two foundational commitments of **cognitive linguistics**. Represents the view that the principles of linguistic structure should reflect what is known about human cognition from other disciplines, particularly the other cognitive sciences (philosophy, psychology, artificial intelligence and neuroscience). It follows from the cognitive commitment that language and linguistic organisation should reflect general cognitive principles rather than cognitive principles that are specific to language. This commitment, central to and definitional of cognitive linguistics, leads to the **generalisation commitment** and the rejection by cognitive linguists of the **modular approach** to language and the mind adopted in **formal linguistics**.

cognitive economy Relates to the way in which human categorisation works so as to provide a maximally efficient way of representing information about frequently encountered objects. Cognitive economy is often stated in terms of the probabilistic notion **cue validity**. Cue validity is maximised at the **basic level**, because basic level categories share the largest number of attributes possible while minimising the extent to which these features are shared by other categories. This means that basic level categories simultaneously maximise the amount of detail they include in their representations (their 'level of inclusiveness'), while maximising their distinctiveness from other categories. This results in optimal cognitive conomy. (See also **prototype, Prototype Theory**.)

Cognitive Grammar The theoretical framework associated with *Ronald Langacker* which has been under development since the mid-1970s and is best represented in his two *Foundations of Cognitive Grammar* volumes published in 1987 and 1991 respectively. This is also the most detailed and comprehensive theory of grammar to have been developed within **cognitive linguistics,** and to date has been the most influential of the **cognitive approaches to grammar.**

Cognitive Grammar attempts to model the cognitive mechanisms and principles that motivate and license the formation and use of linguistic units of varying degrees of complexity. Like the **Conceptual Structuring System Approach** developed by *Leonard Talmy* and the group of theories known as **construction grammars,** Langacker argues that grammatical or **closed class forms** are inherently meaningful. Unlike Talmy, he does not assume that **open class forms** and closed class forms represent distinct conceptual subsystems.

Instead, Langacker argues that both types of unit belong within a single structured inventory of conventionalised linguistic units which represents knowledge of language in the mind of the speaker, giving rise to a **lexicon-grammar continuum.** For Langacker, knowledge of language (the mental grammar) is represented in the mind of the speaker as an inventory of symbolic assemblies. The **symbolic assembly,** which can be **simplex** or **complex,** is the basic unit of grammar. Accordingly, Cognitive Grammar subscribes to the **symbolic thesis.** It is only once an expression has been used sufficiently frequently and has undergone **entrenchment:** acquiring the status of a habit or a 'cognitive routine', that it achieves the status of **a linguistic unit.** From this perspective, a linguistic unit is a symbolic entity that is not built compositionally by the language system but is stored and accessed as a whole. Furthermore, the linguistic units represented in the speaker's grammar reflect usage **conventions**. The conventionality of a linguistic unit relates to the idea that linguistic expressions become part of the grammar of a language by virtue of being shared among members of a speech community. Thus conventionality is a matter of degree. For instance, an expression like *dog* is more conventional (shared by more members of the English-speaking community) than an expression like *allophone*, which is shared only by a subset of English speakers with specialist knowledge relating to the study of linguistics. The roles of entrenchment and conventionality in this model of grammar emerge from the **usage-based thesis**. Accordingly, Cognitive Grammar is sometimes referred to as the **usage-based model** of grammar.

The repository of entrenched symbolic assemblies is conceived in Cognitive Grammar as a mental inventory. Yet the contents of this inventory are not stored in a random way. The inventory is structured, and this structure lies in the **relationships between symbolic assemblies**. For example, some units form sub-parts of other units which in turn form sub-parts of other units (for example, morphemes make up words and words make up phrases which in turn make up sentences). This set of interlinking and overlapping relationships is conceived as a structured network, and Langacker presents this in terms of a **network model**. The entities which populate the network of symbolic assemblies are constrained by what Langacker refers to as the **content requirement**.

cognitive lexical semantics An approach to lexical semantics (word-meaning) that assumes the **guiding principles of cognitive semantics**. Key contributors to this approach include *Claudia Brugman, Hubert Cuyckens, Paul Deane, Vyvyan Evans, Dirk Geeraerts, Anette Herskovits, George Lakoff, Andrea Tyler* and *Claude Vandeloise*. (See also **chaining, cognitive semantics, over, semantic network**.)

cognitive linguistics (also **cognitive linguistics enterprise**) A school of linguistics and cognitive science which emerged from the early 1980s onwards. Places central importance on the role of meaning, conceptual processes and **embodied experience** in the study of language and the mind and the way in which they intersect. Cognitive linguistics is an enterprise or an approach to the study of language and the mind rather than a single articulated theoretical framework. It is informed by two overarching principles or commitments: the **generalisation commitment** and the **cognitive commitment**. The two best developed sub-branches of cognitive linguistics are **cognitive semantics** and **cognitive approaches to grammar**. While cognitive linguistics began to emerge in the 1980s as a broadly grounded intellectual movement, it traces its roots to work that was taking place in the 1970s, particularly in the United States, which was reacting to **formal linguistics**. Early pioneers in the 1970s who were instrumental in formulating this new approach include *Gilles Fauconnier, Charles Fillmore, George Lakoff, Ronald Langacker* and *Leonard Talmy*.

cognitive linguistics enterprise see **cognitive linguistics**

cognitive model A central construct in **LCCM Theory**. Cognitive models, while related to the notion of **frame**, **semantic frame** and **domain (1)**, are distinct from all three. The distinct notion of cognitive model is necessary for understanding the way lexical concepts contribute to meaning construction. The main claim is that a given **lexical concept** provides an **access site** to cognitive models and are relativised with respect to them. A cognitive model is a coherent, in large-part non-linguistic, knowledge structure. That is, it is a richly specified conceptual entity which represents an interface between richly specified conceptual knowledge and nodes of access at particular points in the cognitive model provided by specific lexical concepts. Thus lexical concepts provide particular established (i.e. conventional) perspectives or construals with respect to the set of cognitive models: the **cognitive model profile**, accessed via a given lexical concept.

Cognitive models relate to coherent bodies of knowledge of any kind, being multi-modal conceptual entities, which can be used as a basis for perceptual **simulation**. For instance, they include knowledge relating to specific entities, such as the complex knowledge associated with a 'car', or a more specific entity such as 'my car'. They include information such as whether the car needs filling up and when I last cleaned its interior. Cognitive models can relate to 'procedural' bodies of knowledge such as 'cultural scripts' which form templates for how to interact in restaurants in order to be seated and secure a meal, for instance. Cognitive models also include bodies of knowledge relating to more abstract entities such as containment, love and physics. They operate at varying levels of detail and while stable, are dynamic, being in a perpetual state of modification and renewal by virtue of ongoing experience, mediated both by linguistic and non-linguistic interaction with others and one's environment.

cognitive model profile A theoretical construct in **LCCM Theory**. Refers to the set of cognitive models to which a given **lexical concept** affords **access**. The **cognitive model** profile serves to provide the **semantic potential** from which, in conjunction with processes of **lexical concept integration, conceptual structure** is selected, contributing to the emergence of a **conception**.

By way of illustrating the relationship between a lexical concept and its cognitive model profile, consider the lexical concept [FRANCE]; note that a lexical concept is glossed using small capitals in square brackets. This lexical concept provides access to a large number of cognitive models – its cognitive model profile – at a particular **access site**, which is to say a particular point in the cognitive model profile. A very partial cognitive model profile for this lexical concept is provided in Figure 4. In Figure 4, the lexical concept [FRANCE] provides access to a potentially large number of knowledge structures. As each cognitive model consists of structured knowledge providing access to other sorts of knowledge, we can distinguish between cognitive models which are directly accessed via the lexical concept and those cognitive models which form substructures of the directly accessed cognitive models. That is, such 'secondary' models are indirectly accessed via the lexical concept. Accordingly, a cognitive model profile is a structured inventory of knowledge which lexical concepts afford access to.

For instance, the directly accessed cognitive models include (at the very least) the following: GEOGRAPHICAL LANDMASS, NATION STATE and HOLIDAY DESTINATION. Each of these cognitive models provides access to a sophisticated and large body of knowledge. In Figure 4 a flavour of this is given by virtue of the various 'secondary' cognitive models which are accessed via the NATION STATE cognitive model. These include NATIONAL SPORTS, POLITICAL SYSTEM and

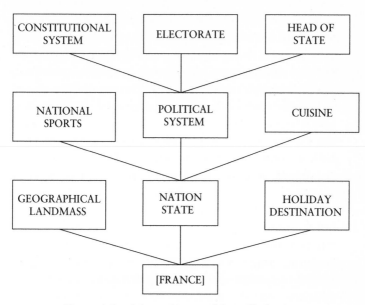

Figure 4. Partial cognitive model profile for [FRANCE]

CUISINE. For instance, we may know that in France, the French engage in national sports of particular types, for instance football, rugby, athletics and so on, and take part in competitions of various kinds including the FIFA football World Cup, the Six Nations rugby competition and the Rugby World Cup, the Olympics and so on. That is, we may have access to a large body of knowledge concerning the sorts of sports French people engage in. We may also have some knowledge of the funding structures and social and economic conditions and constraints that apply to these sports in France, France's international standing in these particular sports and further knowledge about the sports themselves including the rules that govern their practice, and so on. This knowledge is derived from a large number of sources.

With respect to the indirectly accessed cognitive model of POLITICAL SYSTEM, Figure 4 illustrates a sample of further cognitive models which are accessed via this cognitive model. In other words, each 'secondary' cognitive model has further secondary cognitive models which it provides access to. For instance, (FRENCH) ELECTORATE is a cognitive model accessed via the cognitive model (FRENCH) POLITICAL SYSTEM. In turn the cognitive model (FRENCH) POLITICAL SYSTEM is accessed via the cognitive model NATION STATE.

cognitive poetics An approach to the study of literature which applies ideas, constructs and methodology from **cognitive linguistics**. One of the most influential pioneers in cognitive poetics is *Mark Turner*.

cognitive representation (also **CR**) A term coined by **Leonard Talmy**, similar in nature to the notion of the **conceptual system**. In Talmy's **Conceptual Structuring System Approach** the **language user** employs linguistic resources specialised for encoding and externalising his/her cognitive representation.

cognitive semantics The area of study known as cognitive semantics is concerned with investigating the relationship between experience, the **conceptual system** and the **semantic structure** encoded by language. In specific terms, scholars working in cognitive semantics investigate **conceptual structure** (knowledge representation) and **conceptualisation** (meaning construction). Cognitive semanticists have employed language as the lens through which these cognitive phenomena can be investigated. Consequently, research in cognitive semantics tends to be interested in modelling the human mind as much as it is concerned with investigating linguistic semantics.

Like the larger enterprise of **cognitive linguistics** of which it forms a subset, cognitive semantics represents an approach rather than a single articulated theory. There are four **guiding principles of cognitive semantics** that characterise the approach. Some examples of theories in cognitive semantics include **Blending Theory, Conceptual Metaphor Theory, Frame Semantics, Mental Spaces Theory, LCCM Theory, Principled Polysemy** and approaches to linguistic semantics such as **cognitive lexical semantics** and **encyclopaedic semantics**.

communicative intention The second important aspect of the human **intention-reading ability**, central to first language acquisition, involves the recognition of communicative intention. This happens when the child recognises that others are intentional agents and that language represents a special kind of intention: the intention to communicate. For example, when the adult says *rubber duck*, the adult is identifying the toy that is the joint focus of attention and is employing this linguistic symbol to express the intention that the child follow the attention of the adult. (See also **joint attention frame, pattern-finding ability, role reversal imitation, socio-cognitive mechanisms in language acquisition**.)

completion (also known as **pattern completion**) In **Blending Theory**, one of the three component processes that give rise to **emergent structure**. Completion involves **schema induction**: the recruitment of background frames. These complete the **composition**. For instance, in the CLINTON AS FRENCH PRESIDENT **integration**

network, which is prompted by the utterance: *In France, Clinton wouldn't have been harmed by his affair with Monica Lewinsky*, the process of completion introduces the frames for FRENCH POLITICS and FRENCH MORAL ATTITUDES. (For discussion of this blend see the entry for **conceptual integration**.) Without the structure provided by these frames, we would lose the central inference emerging from the blend, which is that Clinton's affair with Lewinsky would not harm Clinton in France. This process of schema induction is called 'completion' because structure is recruited to 'fill out' or complete the information projected from the inputs in order to derive the emergent structure in the blended space. (See also **completion, constitutive principles, elaboration (1), frame.**)

complex Refers to a **symbolic assembly** which contains smaller symbolic assemblies as subparts. Complex symbolic assemblies vary according to the level of complexity, from words (for example, *dogs*) and phrases (for example, *John's brown dog*) to whole sentences (for example, *Geoff kicked the dog*). (See also **Cognitive Grammar, construction (2), simplex.**)

complex atemporal relations A sub-category of **atemporal relations**. A complex atemporal relation encodes a complex static scene, as in the following example: *the sand all over the floor*. What makes this scene 'complex' is that it involves a **multiplex trajector**. (See also **simple atemporal relations.**)

complex metaphor see **compound metaphor**

complex temporal relations A sub-category of **temporal relations**. Complex temporal relations like **simple**

temporal relations involve a process, and hence a temporal relation, because they construe scenes that hold over a given span of time. However, a complex temporal relation designates a dynamic process involving change over time, as illustrated by the following example: *Max is eating the chocolate*.

composite prototype A **prototype** derived from two or more **ICMs** providing highly schematic information. A composite prototype can give rise to further variants established via convention, and thus provides **prototype structure** for a **radial category**. The composite prototype for the category MOTHER, for instance, includes a female who gave birth to the child, was supplier of 50 per cent of the genetic material, stayed at home in order to nurture the child, is married to the child's father, is one generation older than the child and is also the child's legal guardian. Thus the composite prototype draws upon information from a number of distinct ICMs associated with the **cluster model** for MOTHER including: the BIRTH MODEL, the GENETIC MODEL, the NURTURANCE MODEL, the MARITAL MODEL, the GENEALOGICAL MODEL and the HOUSEWIFE-MOTHER MODEL.

composition In **Blending Theory,** one of the three component processes that give rise to **emergent structure.** For instance, in the CLINTON AS FRENCH PRESIDENT **integration network,** due to the utterance: *In France, Clinton wouldn't have been harmed by his affair with Monica Lewinsky*, composition brings together the value BILL CLINTON with the role FRENCH PRESIDENT in the blended space, resulting in the emergent structure: CLINTON AS FRENCH PRESIDENT. See the entry for **conceptual integration** where this blend is described in detail. (See also **completion, constitutive principles, elaboration (1)**.)

compound metaphor (also known as **complex metaphor**) In **Primary Metaphor Theory**, a compound metaphor is a **metaphor** formed by **unification** of more primitive primary metaphors. In other words, while a **primary metaphor** relates two 'simple' concepts from distinct domains, in contrast, compound metaphors relate entire complex domains of experience. A celebrated example of a compound metaphor is THEORIES ARE BUILDINGS, as evidenced by an example such as: *Your theory lacks a solid foundation.* Since both THEORIES and ARGUMENTS are relatively complex and rich in detail, they do not qualify as a **primary target concept** nor a **primary source concept** respectively.

compression In an **integration network,** the process which operates on a **vital relation.** Compression constitutes the process whereby an **outer-space relation** holding between **counterparts** in distinct **input spaces** is 'shortened' so as to 'tighten' the connection between counterparts. This results in **emergent structure,** an **inner-space relation** in the **blended space.** (See also **Blending Theory, decompression.**)

conceived time A term coined by *Ronald Langacker* to refer to the cognitive representation of TIME, where time is an object of **conceptualisation.** Conceived time contrasts with the notion of **processing time.** Langacker argues that there are two types of conceived time, depending upon how events are accessed or processed: these are **sequential scanning** and **summary scanning.**

concept (also **representation**) The fundamental unit of knowledge central to **categorisation** and **conceptualisation**. Concepts inhere in the **conceptual system**, and from early in infancy are redescribed from perceptual experience through a process termed **perceptual meaning analysis**. This process gives rise to the most rudimentary of concepts known as an **image schema**. Concepts can be encoded in a language-specific format know as the **lexical concept**. While concepts are relatively stable cognitive entities they are modified by ongoing episodic and recurrent experiences. (See also **conceptualising capacity, conceptual structure**.)

conception In **LCCM Theory**, the meaning associated with an **utterance**. A conception emerges due to the processes of **lexical concept integration** guided by context and the processes of **backstage cognition**.

conceptual alternativity A term coined by *Leonard Talmy*. Relates to the ability to conceptualise a member of one domain, for instance TIME, in terms of another, for instance SPACE. Conceptual alternativity is facilitated by a **conceptual conversion operation** and is encoded by a given **linguistic unit** such as **closed class forms**.

conceptual archetype A term employed in **Cognitive Grammar**. Refers to a **concept** that has a direct experiential basis but which constitutes an abstraction representing commonalities over ubiquitous everyday experiences. Conceptual archetypes include concepts such as the following: the human body, the human face, a discrete physical object, an object moving through space, the use of one instrument to affect another, one person giving an object to a recipient and so on. Conceptual archetypes form the basis for the category **prototype** of grammatical notions of various kinds. For instance, while the grammatical subject is characterised as the clause-level **trajector** in a **profiled relationship**, the conceptual archetype of AGENT defines the category prototype.

Conceptual Blending Theory see **Blending Theory**

conceptual content system One of two systems within *Leonard Talmy*'s **Conceptual Structuring System Approach**. The conceptual content system provides the rich meaning supported by the **conceptual structuring system**. The meaning associated with the conceptual content system is **content meaning**, which is encoded by **open class forms**.

conceptual conversion operation The mechanism whereby the phenomenon of **conceptual alternativity** is achieved in **homologous categories**. One kind of conceptual conversion operation is **reification**.

conceptual domain see **domain (2)**

conceptual integration (also known as **blending**) The process that results in the formation of a **blended space** in an **integration network**, giving rise to **emergent structure**.

To illustrate, consider the following utterance: *In France Clinton wouldn't have been harmed by his affair with Monica Lewinsky*. This utterance prompts for a blended space in which we understand that as President of France, Clinton would not have been harmed politically by his relationship with Lewinsky. The integration network for this expression includes two **input spaces**. One input space contains CLINTON, LEWINSKY and their RELATIONSHIP. This space is structured by the frame AMERICAN POLITICS. In this frame, there is a role for AMERICAN PRESIDENT together with certain attributes associated with this role such as MORAL VIRTUE, a symbol of which is marital fidelity. In this space, marital infidelity causes political harm. In the second input space, which is structured by the **frame** FRENCH POLITICS, there is a role for FRENCH PRESIDENT. In this frame, it is an accepted part of French public life that the President sometimes has a MISTRESS. In this space, marital infidelity does not result in political harm. The two inputs are related by virtue of a **generic space** which contains the generic roles COUNTRY, HEAD OF STATE, SEXUAL PARTNER and CITIZENS. The generic space establishes cross-space **counterparts** in the input spaces. The blended space contains BILL CLINTON and MONICA LEWINSKY, as well as the roles FRENCH PRESIDENT and MISTRESS OF FRENCH PRESIDENT, with which Clinton and Lewinsky are respectively associated. Crucially, the frame that structures the blend is FRENCH POLITICS rather than AMERICAN POLITICS. It follows that in the blend, Clinton is not politically harmed by his marital infidelity. The integration network for this blend is represented in Figure 5.

Conceptual integration has a number of **constitutive principles**, **goals of blending** and **governing principles** that govern the way in which the process of integration occurs. (See also **Blending Theory**.)

Conceptual Integration Theory see **Blending Theory**

Conceptual Metaphor Theory A theoretical framework developed by *George Lakoff* and *Mark Johnson*, but

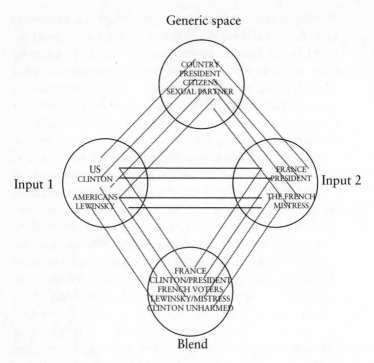

Figure 5. The integration network for CLINTON AS FRENCH
PRESIDENT blend

also associated with other influential scholars including
Zoltán Kövecses, Raymond Gibbs, Eve Sweetser and
Mark Turner. Conceptual Metaphor Theory was first
presented by Lakoff and Johnson in their 1980 volume
Metaphors We Live By. Conceptual Metaphor Theory
was one of the earliest theoretical frameworks to be
developed in **cognitive semantics** and provided much of
the early theoretical impetus for this approach to the
relationship between language, mind and **embodied
experience**. The basic premise of Conceptual Metaphor
Theory is that **metaphor** is not simply a stylistic feature
of language but that thought itself is fundamentally

metaphorical in nature. According to this view, conceptual structure is organised by **cross-domain mappings** or correspondences between conceptual domains. Some of these mappings are due to pre-conceptual embodied experiences while others build on these experiences in order to form more complex conceptual structures. For instance, we can think and talk about the concept of QUANTITY in terms of the concept of VERTICAL ELEVATION, as in *She got a really high mark in the test*, where *high* relates not literally to physical height but to a good mark. According to Conceptual Metaphor Theory, this is because the conceptual **domain (2)** QUANTITY is conventionally structured and therefore understood in terms of the conceptual domain VERTICAL ELEVATION. Conceptual operations involving **mappings**, such as conceptual metaphor, are known more generally as **conceptual projection**. (See also **Primary Metaphor Theory**.)

conceptual metonymy see **metonymy**

conceptual projection Relates to conceptual operations involving **mappings**, such as conceptual **metaphor**, conceptual **metonymy**, **connectors** holding between one **mental space** and another, and processes central to **conceptual integration** such as the **matching** of **counterparts** across **input spaces** and the **compression** of an **outer-space relation** into a **inner-space relation**.

conceptual structure Pertains to knowledge representation, including the structure and organisation of concepts in the human **conceptual system**. Can relate to stable or temporary knowledge structures assembled for purposes of local meaning construction. Cognitive linguists have modelled conceptual structure in terms of relatively stable knowledge structures such as a **domain (1)**, a **cognitive model**, a **semantic frame**, an **idealised cognitive model** and different kinds of **conceptual projection** including cross-domain **mappings** such as **metaphor**. Conceptual structure has also been modelled in terms of **mental space** formation, the establishment of a **mental spaces lattice** and the formation of a conceptual **integration network**. (See also **concept, conceptualisaton, lexical concept**.)

conceptual structuring system One of two systems within *Leonard Talmy's* **Conceptual Structuring System Approach**. The conceptual structuring system provides the structure, skeleton or 'scaffolding' for a given scene, across which the rich substantive detail provided by the **conceptual content system** can be 'draped'. It follows from this that the meaning associated with the conceptual structuring system is **schematic meaning**, as encoded by **closed class forms**. The conceptual structuring system is organised into a number of distinct **schematic systems**, each of which are further divided into **schematic categories**. The four schematic systems are: **configurational system, attentional system, perspectival system** and **force-dynamics system**, a summary of which is presented in Figure 6.

Conceptual Structuring System Approach The approach to grammar developed by *Leonard Talmy*. Like other cognitive approaches to grammar Talmy assumes the **symbolic thesis** and thus treats grammatical units as being inherently meaningful. However, Talmy's model is distinguished by its emphasis on the qualitative distinction between **closed class forms** (grammatical subsystem) and **open class forms** (lexical subsystem). Talmy argues that these two forms of

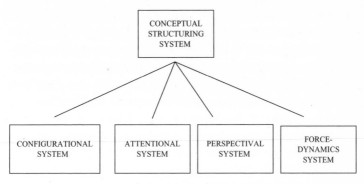

Figure 6. The Conceptual Structuring System

linguistic expression represent two distinct conceptual subsystems which encode qualitatively distinct aspects of the human **conceptual system**. These are the **conceptual structuring system** and the **conceptual content system**. While closed class forms encode **schematic meaning** and constitute the conceptual structuring system, open class elements encode meanings that are far richer in terms of content, **content meaning**, and thus constitute the conceptual content system. In his research, Talmy is primarily interested in delineating the nature and organisation of the conceptual structuring system. In particular, Talmy is concerned with establishing the nature and function of the conceptual structuring system as encoded by closed class elements. For Talmy this issue is a particularly fascinating one as in principle, language could function with a lexical or conceptual content system alone. The fact that languages do not makes establishing the distinction in terms of the respective contributions of the two subsystems in encoding and externalising our **cognitive representation** a particularly intriguing one. (See also **schematic systems.**)

conceptual system The repository of concepts available to a human being. The repository constitutes a structured and organised inventory which facilitates **categorisation** and **conceptualisation**. Each **concept** in the conceptual system can, in principle, be encoded and externalised via language. Concepts encoded in language take a modality-specific format known as a **lexical concept**. Cognitive linguists assume that language reflects the conceptual system and thus can be employed in order to investigate conceptual organisation; they also assume that linguistic organisation which is modified due to use can influence the nature and make-up of the conceptual system. (See also **conceptual structure, conceptualising capacity, usage-based model.**)

conceptualisation The process of meaning construction to which language contributes. It does so by providing **access** to rich **encyclopaedic knowledge** and by prompting for complex processes of **conceptual integration**. Conceptualisation relates to the nature of dynamic thought to which language can contribute. From the perspective of **cognitive linguistics**, linguistic units such as words do not 'carry' meaning(s), but contribute to the process of meaning construction which takes place at the conceptual level. (See also **conceptual structure, conceptual system, conceptualising capacity, level C.**)

conceptualising capacity A common capacity, shared by all humans, to generate concepts, which derives from fundamental and shared aspects of human cognition. Rather than positing universal linguistic principles, cognitive linguists posit a common set of cognitive abilities which serve to both facilitate and constrain the development of our **conceptual system**.

conceptually autonomous The property of being independently meaningful which is associated with **nominal predications**. For instance, expressions such as *bed* or *slipper* invoke concepts that are independently meaningful. The property of being conceptually autonomous contrasts with concepts which are **conceptually dependent**.

conceptually dependent The property associated with **relational predications** which rely on other concepts in order to have their meaning completed. For example, in a sentence such as: *Max hid his mum's mobile phone under the bed*, the verb *hid* relates the **conceptually autonomous** entities MAX, MUM'S MOBILE PHONE and BED, establishing a relationship involving 'hiding' between them. Similarly, *under* establishes a spatial relation between MUM'S MOBILE PHONE and BED.

configurational system One of the four **schematic systems** which form part of the **conceptual structuring system**. The configurational system imposes structure upon the contents of the domains of SPACE and TIME. This is achieved by virtue of six **schematic categories: plexity, dividedness, boundedness, degree of extension, pattern of distribution, axiality**. These categories structure the scenes encoded by language and the participants that interact within these scenes. (See also **attentional system, Conceptual Structuring System Approach, force-dynamics system, perspectival system, schematic categories**.)

connectors In **Mental Spaces Theory**, the cognitive link that holds between elements in distinct mental spaces that are **counterparts**. Connectors represent a special kind of **conceptual projection**.

For instance, elements in different mental spaces that are coreferential, which is to say are related by identity, are linked by an 'identity' connector. To illustrate, consider the following example: *James Bond is a top British spy. In the war, 007 was an officer in the Royal Navy*. In this example, each sentence sets up its own **mental space**. In the first sentence the expression James Bond prompts for the assignment of an element relating to James Bond. In the second sentence the expression *007* prompts for the assignment of the element 007 in the second mental space. Background knowledge tells us that 007 is the code name conventionally assigned to James Bond. This knowledge serves to establish an identity connector linking the elements in the two distinct mental spaces. This is set out in diagrammatic form in Figure 7 where the circles represent distinct mental spaces and the elements in each, James Bond (a_1) and 007 (a_2), are linked by an identity connector, signalled by the line relating a_1 and a_2. (See also **element, property**.)

constitutive processes The processes which together give rise to the formation of an **integration network** and consequently a **blended space**. These include: (1) the construction of a **generic space**; (2) the **matching** of **counterparts** in **input spaces**; (3) **selective projection** of structure from the input spaces; (4) **conceptual integration** in order to form a blended space; (5) which involves the development of **emergent structure** due to the processes of **composition, completion** and **elaboration (1)**. (See also **Blending Theory**.)

construal An idea central to **Cognitive Grammar**. Relates to the way a **language user** chooses to 'package' and 'present' a conceptual representation as encoded in

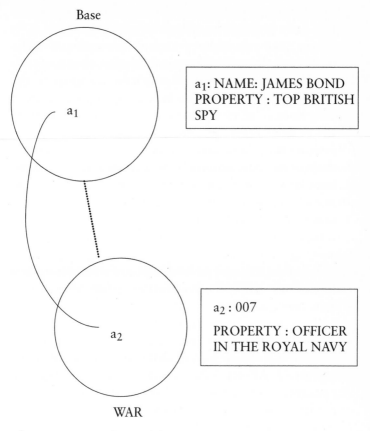

Base

a₁: NAME: JAMES BOND
PROPERTY : TOP BRITISH
SPY

a₂ : 007

PROPERTY : OFFICER
IN THE ROYAL NAVY

WAR

Figure 7. A cross-space connector

language, which in turn has consequences for the conceptual representation that the **utterance** evokes in the mind of the hearer. This is achieved by choosing a particular **focal adjustment** and thus linguistically 'organising' a scene in a specific way. In so doing, the speaker imposes a unique construal upon that scene. For example, the active construction focuses attention upon the AGENT of an action (e.g. *Max hid Angela's* *keys*), while the passive construction focuses attention upon the PATIENT (e.g. *Angela's keys were hidden by Max*). Each of these constructions conventionally encodes a distinct construal. (See also **objective construal, subjective construal**.)

constructicon The term given to the mental inventory of constructions in *Adele Goldberg's* theory of **Construction Grammar (2)**. As Goldberg makes no distinction between **simplex** and **complex** symbolic assemblies (since either kind may count as a **construction (1)** in her theory, in contrast to **Cognitive Grammar**), the constructicon is her term for the **lexicon-grammar continuum**. (See also **construction (2), symbolic assembly**.)

construction (1) A unit of language and the central theoretical construct in **construction grammars**. A construction constitutes a conventional unit pairing form and meaning. Form typically concerns a particular phonological string of sound segments conventional in a particular language, e.g. [kaet] in English. Meaning relates to a mental representation, namely a **lexical concept**, conventionally associated with a form. Hence, [kaet] is conventionally associated with the concept of a kind of animal which is often treated as a domesticated pet in many parts of the world. Thus the **linguistic unit** *cat* constitutes a construction, being comprised of a conventional pairing of form and meaning.

   In addition to whole words, constructions may be a meaningful sub-part of a word, or morpheme (*anti-dis-establish*. . . .), a string of words that 'belong' together, as in an **idiom** such as: *He kicked the bucket*, or 'syntactic constructions' which have more **schematic meaning** associated with them. For instance, the

ditransitive construction has the following syntax: NP1 VERB NP2 NP3, and the schematic meaning: X CAUSES Y TO RECEIVE Z. Such constructions are not **lexically filled,** but represent a grammatical schema which can be instantiated with particular words as in the following sentence: *John gave Mary the flowers.* (See also **construction grammars, constructional meaning, constructional polysemy, constructional profiling, lexicon-grammar continuum, relationships between constructions, symbolic assembly.**)

Construction (2) In **Cognitive Grammar,** a construction refers to a **symbolic assembly** which is **complex** as opposed to **simplex** in nature.

Construction Grammar (1) A theory of grammar developed by *Charles Fillmore, Paul Kay* and their collaborators. While this theory is broadly generative in orientation, it set the scene for the development of cognitively realistic theories of construction grammar which adopted the central thesis of Fillmore and Kay's approach. This thesis is the position that grammar can be modelled in terms of constructions rather than 'words and rules'. Thus Fillmore and Kay developed the **symbolic thesis** as the basis for a theory of grammar. In particular, Construction Grammar is motivated by the fact that certain complex grammatical constructions, in particular **idiomatic expressions** such as *kick the bucket or throw in the towel,* have meaning that cannot be predicted on the basis of their sub-parts and might therefore be 'stored whole' rather than 'built from scratch'. Fillmore and Kay authored two classic Construction Grammar papers which presented case studies of the **let alone construction** and the **What's X doing Y construction.**

One of the notable features of Construction Grammar is that this model is 'monostratal': containing only one level of syntactic representation rather than a sequence of structures linked by transformations: a feature that characterises theories of grammar in formal linguistics such as generative models of grammar. Furthermore, the representations in Construction Grammar contain not only syntactic information but also semantic information relating to **argument structure** as well as pragmatic information. (See also **construction grammars**.)

Construction Grammar (2) A theory of Construction Grammar developed by *Adele Goldberg* which has its roots in the theory of **Construction Grammar (1)** developed by *Charles Fillmore, Paul Kay* and their various collaborators, and is also influenced by the work of *George Lakoff*. In her model, Goldberg developed the constructional approach of Fillmore and Kay by extending it from 'irregular' **idiomatic expressions** to 'regular' constructions. In order to do this, she focused on **verb argument constructions**. In other words, she examined 'ordinary' sentences, such as ones with transitive or ditransitive structure, and built a theory of construction grammar to account for the **argument structure** patterns she found there. In so doing, one of Goldberg's notable achievements was to apply received ideas from **cognitive semantics**, such as **polysemy** and **metaphor**, and incorporate them in a new theory of Construction Grammar. Thus her approach reveals that grammar exhibits the same sorts of phenomena as other linguistic units such as words. Accordingly, Goldberg's Construction Grammar posited a **lexicon-grammar continuum**, which she refers to as the **constructicon**. (See also **construction grammars**.)

construction grammars A set of **cognitive approaches to grammar** which assume that the **construction** (1) is the fundamental unit of grammar. There are several distinct varieties of construction grammars including: *Fillmore and Kay's* **Construction Grammar** (1), *Goldberg's* **Construction Grammar** (2), **Embodied Construction Grammar** and **Radical Construction Grammar**. (See also **guiding principles of cognitive approaches to grammar**.)

constructional meaning The idea, associated with the family of **construction grammars**, that a **construction** (1) has a conventional meaning associated with it. (See also **caused motion construction, intransitive construction, let alone construction, resultative construction, What's X doing Y? construction**.)

constructional polysemy The view in **Construction Grammar** (2) that a **construction** (1), just like a word, exhibits **polysemy**. Consider the following examples of the **ditransitive construction**:

1. Max gave Bella a biscuit
2. Angela knitted Bella a jumper
3. John owes me a fiver

While each of these examples has to do with TRANSFER, they each differ in subtle but important ways. Example (1) implies SUCCESSFUL TRANSFER of *a biscuit* to *Bella* while example (2) only implies INTENDED TRANSFER (it's possible that Angela may never complete the jumper). In (3), we have TRANSFER WHICH DEPENDS ON CERTAIN SATISFACTION CONDITIONS BEING MET: for instance, it depends on John being able to, willing to and/or intending to repay the money. Thus examples such as these are held to provide evidence that the ditransitive construction exhibits polysemy. (See also **Scene Encoding Hypothesis**.)

constructional profiling In **Construction Grammar (2)**, the realisation of **argument roles** in terms of core grammatical relations (subject, direct object or indirect object). Other argument roles may optionally be present in the sentence but represented as prepositional phrases, sometimes called 'oblique' objects. For instance, in the example: *The thief opened the window with the crowbar*, the argument roles AGENT and PATIENT lexicalised by *the thief* and *the window* respectively are constructionally profiled as they are associated with a 'direct' grammatical relation: subject and object. However, the argument role INSTRUMENT lexicalised by *the crowbar* is not constructionally profiled as it is not associated with a 'direct' grammatical relational but rather is introduced by a preposition and thus constitutes an 'oblique' object.

content function see **content meaning**

content meaning (also **content function**) The kind of meaning associated with elements in the **conceptual content system**, as encoded by **open class forms**. Meaning of this kind is rich in nature and thus contrasts with the meaning associated with elements in the **conceptual structuring system** as encoded by **closed class forms**. Content meaning relates to concepts having to do with things, people, places, events, properties of things and so on. For instance, compare the following two sentences:

1. **The** movie star kiss**ed the** directors.
2. **The** sunbeam illumina**ted the** rooftops.

The grammatical structure of these two sentences is identical (the closed class or 'grammatical' words are highlighted in bold). For instance, both participants in the events described by these sentences can easily be identified by the hearer; the event took place before now; there's only one movie star/ sunbeam but more than one director/rooftop. Yet the sentences differ in a rather dramatic way. They no longer describe the same kind of event at all. This is because the open class forms (unbolded in these sentences) prompt for certain kinds of concepts that are richer and less schematic in nature. That is, the unbolded elements are associated with content meaning.

content requirement A constraint proposed by *Ronald Langacker* which places limits on how the theory of **Cognitive Grammar** operates. This requirement holds that the only entities permissible within the grammar of a language are: (1) phonological, semantic and symbolic units; (2) the relations that hold between them; and (3) the schemas that represent these units. This requirement excludes abstract rules from the model, in contrast to theories of grammar in **formal linguistics**. Instead, knowledge of any given linguistic pattern is conceived in terms of a **schema**. (See also **symbolic assembly, symbolic thesis**.)

contextual modulation A term coined by *Alan Cruse*. Relates to the fact that in ordinary speech the meaning associated with a lexical item undergoes 'modulation' as a result of the context in which it is used. For instance, in the following examples, the semantic contribution of *fast* is adjusted as a consequence of the context in which it is embedded:

1. That parked BMW is a fast car
2. That BMW is travelling fast
3. That's the fast lane of the motorway

In the example in (1), *fast* relates to the potential for rapid locomotion. In (2) *fast* relates to rapid locomotion. In (3) *fast* relates to a venue for rapid locomotion.

contrast set A notion developed within the theory of **Principled Polysemy** as applied to prepositions. Certain clusters of prepositions appear to pattern as a system serving to divide up various spatial dimensions. For example, *above*, *over*, *under* and *below* form a contrast set that divides the vertical dimension of space into four related subspaces, as illustrated in Figure 8.

As Figure 8 shows, *over* and *under* tend to refer to those subspaces along the vertical axis that are physically closer to the **landmark**, while *above* and *below* tend to designate relations in which the **trajector** is further away from the landmark. In the figure, the bold horizontal line represents the landmark, while the dotted lines refer to areas of vertical space higher and lower than the landmark which count as proximal. The dark circles represent trajectors in each subspace, corresponding to the prepositions listed on the left of the diagram.

conventional blend A cognitive entity that while having emerged via the dynamic processes of **conceptual integration** has nevertheless become relatively well established in a particular linguistic community. Consequently, the blend is not reconstructed each time it is prompted for but is conventionalised as a 'pre-assembled' cognitive routine. An example of

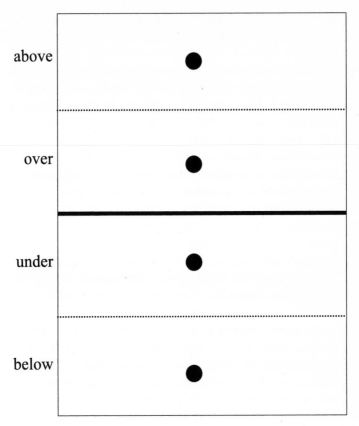

Figure 8. A prepositional contrast set

a conventional blend is the GRIM REAPER blend discussed in the entry for **megablend**. (See also **Blending Theory**.)

conventional mappings see **cross-domain mappings**

conventions The 'norms' of linguistic behaviour in a particular linguistic community. These include, among other things, lexical forms, grammatical patterns, supra-segmental phonology and discourse strategies.

correlation-based metaphor A **metaphor** based on tight and recurring correlations or co-occurrences in experience rather than being motivated by perceived similarity or resemblance between two entities. Correlation-based metaphor thus contrasts with **resemblance-based metaphor**. An example of a correlation-based metaphor is INTIMACY IS WARMTH as evidenced by the expression: *Those two have a warm relationship*. As intimacy co-varies with warmth in experience, INTIMACY and WARMTH are tightly correlated. This is held to give rise to a conceptual association at the cognitive level between intimacy and warmth thus establishing the conceptual metaphor: INTIMACY IS WARMTH.

Correspondence Principle One of the two principles that facilitate **fusion (1)** in **Construction Grammar (2)**. The Correspondence Principle governs **constructional profiling** as it relates to the integration of **argument roles** and **participant roles**. The Correspondence Principle states that profiled argument roles are obligatorily matched with profiled participant roles, but builds some flexibility into the system by allowing that one of the participant roles may or may not be constructionally profiled in the case of a verb with three participant roles. Equally, the **ditransitive construction** can contribute a third argument role to a two-participant verb.

counterparts In **Mental Spaces Theory**, elements in different mental spaces that are linked by **connectors**. Counterparts are established on the basis of 'pragmatic function'. That is, when two (or more) elements in different mental spaces have a related pragmatic function, they are counterparts. One salient type of pragmatic function is 'identity'. For instance, in Ian Fleming's novels, *James Bond* is the name of the fictional British spy character and *007* is the code name used by the British Secret Service (MI6) to identify this spy. The pragmatic function relating the entities referred to as *James Bond* and *007* is coreference or identity. In other words, both expressions refer to the same individual and together form a 'chain of reference'.

To illustrate this, consider the following example: *James Bond is a top British spy. In the war, 007 was an officer in the Royal Navy.* In this example, each sentence sets up its own **mental space**. In the first sentence the expression James Bond prompts for the assignment of an element relating to James Bond. In the second sentence the expression *007* prompts for the assignment of the element 007 in the second mental space. Background knowledge tells us that 007 is the code name conventionally assigned to James Bond. This knowledge provides a pragmatic function which serves to establish the two elements as counterparts. This is set out in diagrammatic form in Figure 9 where the circles represent distinct mental spaces and the elements in each, James Bond (a_1) and 007 (a_2), are linked by an identity connector, signalled by the line relating a_1 and a_2, and are thus counterparts. (See also **element, property**.)

CR see **cognitive representation**

cross-domain mappings The species of **mappings** central to **Conceptual Metaphor Theory**. Mappings of this kind persist in long-term memory and serve to structure one conceptual **domain (2)**, the **target domain**, in

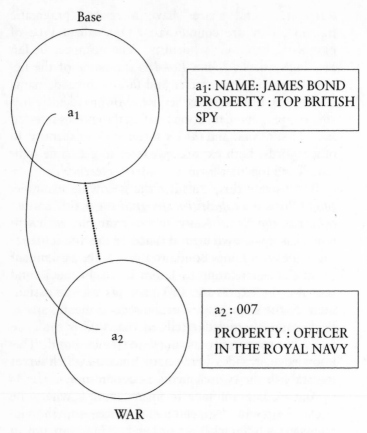

Figure 9. Counterparts across mental spaces

terms of another domain, the **source domain.** Cross-domain mappings are held to provide one of the key ways in which the **conceptual system** is organised. According to Conceptual Metaphor Theory, it is due to the existence of cross-domain mappings that we can think and talk about one domain, for instance the domain of QUANTITY in terms of another domain, for instance the domain of VERTICALITY. This is evidenced

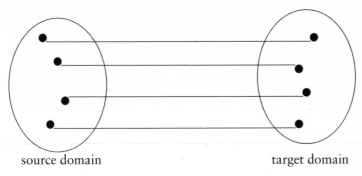

source domain   target domain

Figure 10. Cross-domain mappings

by an example such as *She got a really high mark in the test*. In this example, *high* relates not literally to physical height but to a good mark. That is, we understand quantity in terms of height due to a conventional association between the two domains facilitated by long-term cross-domain mappings projecting structure from the source domain onto the target domain. In practice cross-domain mappings are conceived of as a stable relationship holding between sets of concepts belonging to two distinct domains, as set out diagrammically in Figure 10.

In this diagram the small black circles represent concepts and the connecting lines represent cross-domain mappings. A set of cross-domain mappings holding between two distinct conceptual domains is referred to as a conceptual **metaphor**.

cue validity A probabilistic concept developed in **Prototype Theory**. Cue validity is a statistical measure which predicts that a particular cue – or attribute – becomes more valid or relevant to a given category the more frequently it is associated with members of that category. Conversely, a particular attribute becomes less valid or relevant to a category the more frequently it is associated with members of other categories. Thus, 'is used for sitting on' has 'high cue validity' for the category CHAIR, but 'is found in the home' has low cue validity for the category CHAIR because many other different categories of object can be found in the home in addition to chairs. Cue validity is closely associated with the notion of **cognitive economy**. (See also **basic level, prototype**.)

| D |

debounding A grammatical operation in which a count entity is converted into a mass entity. For instance in the following:

1. I have a tomato
2. After my fall there was tomato all over my face

the count noun *tomato* undergoes a debounding operation by virtue of the grammatical construction *there was* which serves to render *tomato* as a mass noun, a debounded entity. Debounding contrasts with the grammatical operation known as **excerpting**. (See also **Conceptual Structuring System Approach**.)

decoding idioms An expression such as *kick the bucket* that has to be decoded or 'learnt whole'. Decoding idioms are those whose meaning cannot be constructed from the sum of the individual lexical items that constitute the idiom and contrast with **encoding idioms**. (See **Construction Grammar (1)**, **idiomatic expressions**.)

decompression In an **integration network**, the process whereby the emergent structure in the **blended space** is separated, so that the **counterparts** and **outer-space relations** that produced it can be reconstructed. In other words, decompression is the process whereby a highly **conventional blend** can serve to reconstruct the inputs that gave rise to the blended space in the first place. (See also **Blending Theory.**)

degree of extension   One of the **schematic categories** in the **configurational system**. Degree of extension relates to how far quantities of SPACE or TIME 'stretch' over distance. This category interacts with **boundedness**, but introduces a more detailed structure. For example, SPACE or TIME can be either a **point** (*speck, to die*), a **bounded extent** (*ladder, to wash up*) or an **unbounded extent** (*river, to sleep*). Focusing on the domain of TIME, examples (1–3) below illustrate that each of these degrees of extension (encoded by the verb) is compatible with different types of adverbial expressions, given in square brackets.

1. The soldier died [at three o'clock]   [point]
2. Max washed up [in ten minutes]   [bounded extent]
3. Isabella slept [for an hour]   [unbounded extent]

(See also **axiality, boundedness, Conceptual Structuring System Approach, degree of extension, dividedness, pattern of distribution, plexity, schematic systems.**)

direction   One of the four **schematic categories** in the **perspectival system**. This category interacts closely with the **attentional system** and concerns the direction in which an event is viewed relative to a given perspective point. The direction can be 'prospective' or 'retrospective' as illustrated below:

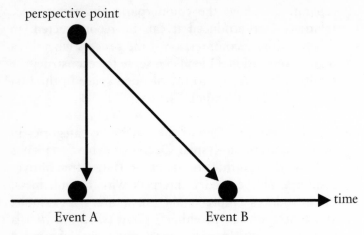

perspective point

Event A

Event B

time

Figure 11. Prospective direction

1. Edith finished the glass of rosé
   before she went home   [prospective]
2. Before she went home, Edith
   finished the glass of rosé   [retrospective]

In these examples, it is not the order of the events themselves that is different; in both cases, Edith first finishes her drink and then goes home. The difference relates to the direction from which the two events are viewed, which is illustrated in the Figures 11 and 12.

In the prospective direction, the event-sequence is viewed from the perspective of the first event, event A. That is, the perspective point is located at the temporally earlier event, from which the speaker looks 'forward' to the later event. In the retrospective direction, the event-sequence is viewed from the perspective of the second event, event B (going home). That is, the perspective point is located at the temporally later event (going home) and the viewing direction is 'backwards',

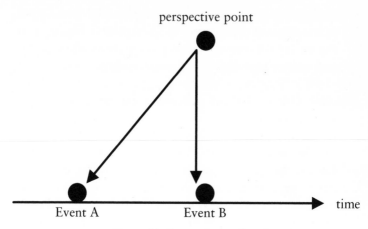

Figure 12. Retrospective direction

towards the earlier event. (See also **conceptual system, direction, distance, location.**)

discourse metaphor A construct developed in the work of *Jörg Zinken*. Discourse metaphors emerge in discourse and are conventionally tied to a particular linguistic form. That is, they are explicitly claimed not to be motivated by an underlying conceptual **metaphor**. In this, the theoretical account of discourse-based metaphors can be seen as standing in opposition to the orthodoxy of Conceptual Metaphor Theory and represents a **usage-based model** of metaphor. Discourse metaphors are associated with particular communicative needs and may often be polemical, dying out when the communicative need they serve is no longer required or relevant. For instance, the discourse metaphor *Frankenfood* was applied to food based on genetically modified crops in European public discourse during the 1990s. The purpose of the metaphor, employed initially in publications by the Friends of the

Earth organisation, was to stigmatise GM-based foods by associating them with the Frankenstein **frame**, relating to an abhorrent man-made creation which led to unforeseen and disastrous consequences.

distance One of the four **schematic categories** in the **perspectival system**. This category relates to distance of a referent relative to a speaker or hearer and is encoded by **closed class forms**. For instance, Hausa, a West African language belonging to the Chadic branch of the Afroasiatic family, exhibits a four-way distance distinction. In this language, demonstrative determiners, pronouns and adverbs are marked for relative distance which can be glossed as follows: 'speaker-proximal', 'addressee proximal', 'speaker/addressee medial' and 'speaker/addressee distal'. (See also **conceptual system, direction, location, mode.**)

distributed spatial semantics An approach to analysing meaning and expression in spatial language developed by *Chris Sinha* and *Tania Kuteva*. This approach starts from the rejection of the assumption that spatial meaning (for instance, path, source, goal and so forth) is 'packaged' by selecting single classes of lexical items. It is often, in fact, assumed that fully specified spatial meaning is expressed universally by closed class grammatical classes such as prepositions. According to the distributed spatial semantics approach, this view is problematic. For instance, the semantic value associated with the English lexical item *in*, as evidenced by examples such as the following, varies: *the coffee in the bowl* versus *the spoon in the cup*. While coffee is enclosed by the cup, the spoon is not wholly enclosed. The distributed spatial semantics approach holds that to assume that variation in meaning of this kind is the result of distinct senses being conventionally associated with a form such as *in* would lead to the **polysemy fallacy**. In contrast, Sinha and Kuteva propose that spatial meaning itself is distributed over several grammatical classes, not only those conventionally considered to have locative meaning such as prepositions. This leads to the general proposition that spatial meaning is characterised by many-to-many mappings between spatial meaning and the particular forms employed to encode the given spatial meaning. In this approach, the mappings may be many-to-one (conflation), one-to-one (compositional) or one-to-many (distribution). Additionally, Sinha and Kuteva argue that there is a typological distinction in the languages of the world in the way in which spatial meaning is distributed. Some languages, for instance Japanese, frequently repeat the same spatial information in different places in the utterance, sometimes using the same morpheme in different grammatical roles. This they refer to as 'overt' distributed spatial semantics. Other languages, including English, tend to compress the spatial meanings, omitting explicit encoding of some parts of it, as in for example *the boy jumped the fence*, where the preposition is optional. This is referred to as 'covert' distributed spatial semantics. (See also **cognitive lexical semantics**.)

ditransitive construction (also **double object construction**)
One of the **verb argument constructions** studied by *Adele Goldberg* in the development of her theory of **Construction Grammar (2)**. The ditransitive construction is associated with the syntactic frame [SUBJ [V OBJ OBJ$_2$]] (*e.g. Paul gave Edith flowers*), where both objects are noun phrases (NPs). There are claimed to be a number of properties that are specific to the

Table 3. Properties of the English ditransitive construction

The English ditransitive construction: X CAUSES Y TO RECEIVE Z

Contributes TRANSFER semantics that cannot be attributed to the lexical verb

The GOAL argument must be animate (RECIPIENT rather than PATIENT)

Two non-predicative NPs are licensed in post-verbal position

The construction links RECIPIENT role with object function

The subject function must be filled with a volitional AGENT, who intends TRANSFER

---

ditransitive construction which cannot be predicted either from the lexical items that fill the construction or from other constructions in the language. These are summarised in Table 3. Crucially the ditransitive, as with other verb argument constructions, is held to exhibit **constructional polysemy**.

dividedness One of the **schematic categories** in the **configurational system**. Dividedness relates to the internal segmentation of a quantity and underlies the distinction between discrete and continuous matter. Discrete matter can be broken down into distinct parts, for instance the categories *timber* and *furniture*, which are made up of discrete entities. Continuous matter cannot be broken down into discrete matter, for instance *oxygen* and *water*. Dividedness overlaps with but is not the same as the schematic category of **boundedness**. For instance, the properties 'unbounded' and 'continuous' are not the same, although they can correlate. While the mass noun *oxygen* is both continuous and unbounded, in contrast the mass noun *furniture* is unbounded but has internally discrete structure. The schematic category dividedness is not encoded by **closed class forms.** (See also **axiality, boundedness, Conceptual Structuring System Approach, degree of extension, pattern of distribution, plexity, schematic systems.**)

domain (1) A conceptual entity posited in **Cognitive Grammar.** A domain constitutes a coherent knowledge structure possessing, in principle, any level of complexity or organisation. For instance, a domain can constitute a **concept,** a **semantic frame** or some other representational space or conceptual complex. Crucially, a domain provides a particular kind of coherent knowledge representation against which other conceptual units such as a concept are characterised. For instance, linguistic terms such as *hot*, *cold* and *lukewarm* relate to different kinds of **lexical concept** which can only be fully characterised with respect to the domain of TEMPERATURE. Hence, the central function of a domain is to provide a relatively stable knowledge context in terms of which other kinds of conceptual units can be understood. (See also **abstract domain, base, basic domain, domain matrix, hierarchy of domain complexity, profile.**)

domain (2) (also **conceptual domain, experiential domain**) A conceptual entity employed in **Conceptual Metaphor Theory** and related approaches to **conceptual projection** such as approaches to conceptual **metonymy** and **primary metaphor theory.** Conceptual domains are relatively complex knowledge structures which relate to coherent aspects of experience. For instance, the conceptual domain JOURNEY is hypothesised to include representations for things such as traveller, mode of transport, route, destination, obstacles encountered on the route and so forth. A conceptual **metaphor** serves to establish correspondences known as **cross-domain mappings** between a **source domain** and a **target domain** by projecting representations from one conceptual domain onto corresponding representations in another conceptual domain.

Domain Highlighting Model A model of lexical and conceptual relations, especially conceptual **metonymy**, built on the **Cognitive Grammar** view of the **domain** (1) and developed by *William Croft*. On this account, a target is accessed within a domain as a result of domain 'highlighting'. Croft's proposal is that, from the perspective of **encyclopaedic semantics**, which is assumed by this model, metonymy functions by highlighting one domain within a concept's **domain matrix**. Thus a particular usage of a **lexical concept** can highlight distinct domains within the concept's domain matrix on different occasions depending on the utterance context. Consider the following examples:

1. Proust spent most of his time in bed
2. Proust is tough to read

Part of the domain matrix associated with Marcel Proust is that he was man known for particular habits relating to how much time he spent in bed. This is knowledge about Proust the man. Another aspect of the domain matrix relates to Proust's literary work and his career as a writer. While the expression *Proust* in (1) highlights the domain for Proust (Proust the man), the expression *Proust* in (2) highlights the literary work of Proust. Thus, from the perspective of domain matrices, a particular expression can metonymically highlight distinct, albeit related, aspects of our encyclopaedic knowledge relating to Proust.

domain matrix The range of possible domains to which a lexical item serves as a point of **access**. For instance, the lexical item *uncle* provides access to a large inventory of domains including, at the very least, the following: GENEALOGY, PERSON, GENDER, SEXUAL INTERCOURSE, BIRTH, LIFE CYCLE, PARENT/CHILD RELATIONSHIP, SIBLING RELATIONSHIP. (See also **base, domain (1), profile, scope of predication.**)

dominion A key idea in the **Cognitive Grammar** account of **reference point** phenomena. The dominion constitutes the possible set of targets that a given reference point can invoke. (See also **target (2).**)

double object construction see **ditransitive construction**

double-scope network A type of **integration network** in which both **input spaces** also contain distinct frames but the **blended space** is organised by structure taken from each **frame,** hence the term 'double-scope'. One consequence of this is that the blend can sometimes include structure from inputs that is incompatible and therefore 'clashes'. It is this aspect of double-scope networks that makes them particularly important, because integration networks of this kind are highly innovative and can lead to novel inferences.

An example of a double-scope network in which the two organising frames clash is prompted for by the following example: *You're digging your own grave.* This idiomatic expression relates to a situation in which someone is doing something foolish that will result in unwitting failure of some kind. For instance, a businessman who is considering taking out a loan that stretches his business excessively might be warned by his accountant that the business risks collapse. At this point, the accountant might say: *You're digging your own financial grave*. This double-scope blend has two input spaces, each structured by a frame: one in which the BUSINESSMAN takes out a LOAN his company can ill afford and another relating to GRAVE DIGGING. Both these frames are projected to the blended space, the loan proves to be excessive and the company fails: the BUSINESSMAN and his BUSINESS end up in a FINANCIAL GRAVE. In this example, the frames projected clash in a number of ways. For example, they clash in terms of causality. While in the BUSINESS input the excessive loan is causally related to failure, in the GRAVE DIGGING input, digging a grave does not cause death; typically it is a response to death. Despite this, in the blended space, digging the grave causes DEATH-AS-BUSINESS FAILURE. Because the accountant's utterance gives rise to the DEATH-AS-BUSINESS FAILURE interpretation, the businessman is able to understand that the loan is excessive and will cause the business to fail. (See also **Blending Theory, mirror network, simplex network, single-scope network.**)

E

ECG see **Embodied Construction Grammar**

ego-based cognitive model for time A temporal reference frame which serves to 'locate' events by virtue of their relationship to the subjective experience of now or the PRESENT. There are two ego-based cognitive models for time in many languages, including English: **moving time model** and **moving ego model**. (See also **time-based cognitive model for time.**)

elaboration (1) (also **running the blend**) In **Blending Theory,** one of the three component processes that give rise to **emergent structure** in the **blended space.** Elaboration is the process whereby structure which emerges due to **composition** and **completion** can be further developed by virtue of a **simulation** in order to develop further new structure. (See also **completion, composition, constitutive principles.**)

Elaboration (2) The idea in **Cognitive Grammar** that the **profile** of a particular expression 'fills in' or completes the meaning of another expression. It does so by combining with a particular **elaboration site** of another expression: the schematic **trajector** or **landmark** of a larger **relational predication.** For instance, consider the expression *under the sofa.* The landmark of *under* is a schematic representation of some **thing** in SPACE. The profile of *the sofa* 'fills in' or elaborates this schematic landmark, and the prepositional phrase as a whole inherits its specificity or **content meaning** from the noun.

elaboration site (also **e-site**) The schematic **trajector** or **landmark** that a particular expression can fill in order to complete an expression via the process known as **elaboration (2).**

element An entity within a **mental space** established by a specific linguistic expression. Elements are entities which can either be constructed on-line in the moment of thinking and speaking or can relate to pre-existing entities in the **conceptual system.** The linguistic expressions that serve to prompt for elements are noun phrases (NPs). These include linguistic expressions like names (*Fred, Elvis, Madonna, Elizabeth Windsor, Tony Blair, James Bond*), descriptions (*the Queen, the*

Prime Minister, a green emerald, a Whitehouse intern, an African elephant), and pronouns (*she, he, they, it*). Elements in distinct mental spaces can serve as counterparts if connectors are established between them. (See also **Mental Spaces Theory, property, relation, role-value readings.**)

embodied cognition (also **thesis of embodied cognition**) One of the guiding principles of **cognitive semantics** and at the heart of much research in **cognitive linguistics**. This thesis holds that the human mind and conceptual organisation are a function of the way in which our species-specific bodies interact with the environment we inhabit. In other words, the nature of concepts and the way they are structured and organised is constrained by the nature of our **embodied experience**. As cognitive linguists hold that language reflects conceptual structure, then it follows that language reflects embodied experience. Scholars who have championed versions of the thesis of embodied cognition include *George Lakoff* and *Mark Johnson* in their work on **metaphor** and the **image schema**, *Ronald Langacker* in his development of **Cognitive Grammar** and *Leonard Talmy* in his investigations on how language encodes conceptual structure (See also **embodiment, situated embodiment, variable embodiment.**)

Embodied Construction Grammar (also **ECG**) Embodied Construction Grammar (ECG) is a recent theory of construction grammar developed by *Benjamin Bergen* and *Nancy Chang* together with various collaborators. In this model, the emphasis is on language processing, particularly language comprehension or understanding. While other construction grammars place the emphasis on modelling linguistic knowledge rather than on on-line processing, the ECG model takes it for granted that constructions form the basis of linguistic knowledge, and focuses instead on exploring how constructions are processed in on-line or dynamic language comprehension. Moreover, ECG is centrally concerned with describing how the constructions of a given language relate to **embodied cognition** in the process of language understanding, and how the constructions of a language give rise to **simulation**. Therefore much of the research to date in ECG has been focused on developing a formal 'language' to describe the constructions of a language like English; this formal language also needs to be able to describe the embodied concepts that these constructions give rise to in dynamic language comprehension.

embodied experience The idea that experience is embodied entails that we have a species-specific view of the world due to the unique nature of our physical bodies. In other words, our **construal** of reality is mediated in large measure by the nature of our bodies.

One example of the way embodiment affects the nature of experience is in the realm of colour. While the human visual system has three kinds of photoreceptors or colour channels, other organisms often have a different number. The visual system of squirrels and rabbits, for instance, makes use of two colour channels, while animals such as goldfish and pigeons have four colour channels. Having a different range of colour channels affects our experience of colour in terms of the range of colours accessible to us along the colour spectrum. Some organisms can see in the infrared range, like rattlesnakes which hunt prey at night and can visually detect the heat given off by other organisms. Humans are unable to see in this range.

Accordingly the visual system – one aspect of our physical embodiment – determines the nature and range of human visual experience. (See also **embodied cognition, embodiment, variable embodiment.**)

embodiment Pertains to the body, especially species-specific physiology and anatomy. Physiology has to do with biological morphology, which is to say body parts and organisation, such as having hands, arms and (bare) skin rather than wings and feathers. Anatomy has to with internal organisation of the body. This includes the neural architecture of an organism, which is to say the brain and nervous system. The notion of embodiment plays an important role in many cognitive linguistic theories. (See **embodied cognition, embodied experience, variable embodiment.**)

EMCL Empirical Methods in Cognitive Linguistics. A workshop series that promotes empirical investigation and methods in **cognitive linguistics**.

emergent grammar A view of grammar associated with *Paul Hopper* which adopts the **usage-based thesis**. According to Hopper, the grammar of a language is not most insightfully conceived as a fixed or stable system that precedes discourse. Rather, he argues that the constructions which make up the grammar are in a continual state of modification, emerging from and being shaped by ongoing discourse as much as they shape discourse. (See also **construction (1)**.)

emergent structure The **conceptual structure** which arises in the **blended space** in an **integration network** due to the process known as **conceptual integration**. The structure is emergent or novel as it is not a property of any of the **input spaces**, taken individually, that comprise an integration network.

To illustrate consider the **metaphoric blend**: *That surgeon is a butcher*. Although butchery is a highly skilled profession, involving considerable expertise and skill including detailed knowledge of the anatomy of particular animals, knowledge of different cuts of meat and so on, by conceptualising a surgeon as a butcher we are evaluating the surgeon as incompetent. **Blending Theory** is able to account for the negative assessment arising from understanding a surgeon in terms of a butcher by allowing for emergent structure. While a blend contains structure projected from both inputs, it also contains additional structure projected from neither. In the input space for BUTCHER, we have a highly skilled professional. However, in the blended space, these skills are inappropriate for performing surgery on human patients. While surgeons attempt to save lives, butchers perform their work on dead animals. While the activity performed by butchers is dismembering, the activity performed by surgeons typically involves repair and reconstruction and so on. The consequence of these contrasts is that in the blended space a surgeon who is assessed as a butcher brings inappropriate skills and indeed goals to the task at hand and is therefore incompetent. This emergent meaning of incompetence represents the additional structure provided by the blend. The emergent structure provided by the blend includes the structure copied from the input spaces together with the emergent structure relating to a surgeon who performs an operation using the skills of butchery and is therefore incompetent. This individual does not exist in either of the input spaces. The structure in the blend is 'emergent' because it emerges from 'adding together'

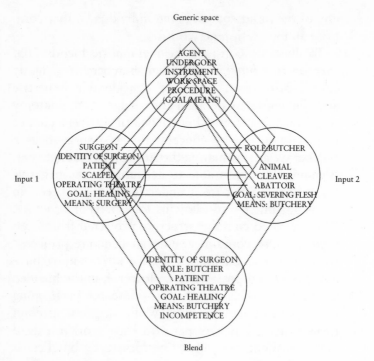

Figure 13. Emergent structure in a metaphoric blend

structure from the inputs to produce an entity unique to the blend. Furthermore, it is precisely by virtue of the mismatch between goal (healing) and means (butchery), which exists only in the blend, that the inference of incompetence arises. This means that all the structure in the blend can be described as emergent, even though its 'ingredients' are provided by the input spaces. The integration network for this blend is given in diagrammatic form in Figure 13.

Emergent structure is a function of three of the **constitutive processes** of blending: **composition, pattern completion** and **elaboration (1)**.

emergentism A view of first language acquisition advocated by *Elizabeth Bates, Michael Tomasello* and others which stands in direct opposition to nativism. This view holds that when children acquire a language, what they are actually doing is acquiring **constructions**: linguistic units of varying sizes and increasing degrees of abstractness. As the complexity and abstractness of the units increases, linguistic creativity begins to emerge. According to this view, the creativity exhibited by young children in their early language happens because they are constructing utterances out of already mastered constructions in ways that facilitate expression of a situated communicative intention. Thus from this perspective the process of language acquisition is 'emergent', involving a huge amount of learning, rather than due to an innate pre-specification for language, a 'universal grammar'.

encoding idioms An example of an encoding idiom is *wide awake*. While idioms of this kind may be understood on first hearing: the adjective *wide* functions as a degree modifier, and while it is possible to work out that this expression means 'completely awake', the speaker would not be able to predict the conventionality of the expression. In other words, there is nothing in the 'rules' of English that enables a speaker to predict that this is the conventional way in which the meaning associated with *wide awake* is encoded, as opposed to, say, *broad awake, big awake, large awake* and so on. Encoding idioms contrast with **decoding idioms**. (See also **Construction Grammar (1), idiomatic expressions**.)

encompassing secondary reference object A kind of secondary reference object. Provides a means, often determined by invariant aspects of the physical environment, of furnishing the **primary reference object** with **axial properties**. This in turn facilitates location of the **figure**. This is achieved by virtue of a reference object which encompasses the **primary reference object** thus providing an absolute 'field' of reference. For instance, in the sentence: *Big Ben is south of the river Thames*, *Big Ben* is the figure, the entity we are attempting to locate, and *the river Thames* is the primary reference object. However, in order to locate Big Ben and establish which side of the river the figure is to be found a secondary reference object is invoked. In this case, the term south invokes the planet Earth as secondary reference object. It is because this particular reference object, the Earth, encompasses the primary reference object that it is referred to as encompassing. (See also **external secondary reference object**.)

encyclopaedic knowledge The structured body of non-linguistic knowledge to which a **linguistic unit** such as a word potentially provides **access**. Encyclopaedic knowledge is modelled in terms of a number of constructs including the **domain (1)**, the **cognitive model** and the **idealised cognitive model**. (See also **encyclopaedic semantics**.)

Encyclopaedic semantics The general approach to linguistic semantics adopted in **cognitive semantics**. There are five key assumptions which comprise this perspective. Firstly, There is no principled distinction between semantics and pragmatics, that is there is no distinction between 'core' meaning on the one hand, and pragmatic, social or cultural meaning on the other. Secondly, **encyclopaedic knowledge** is structured: the knowledge structures that words provide **access** to represent an organised inventory of knowledge. Thirdly, encyclopaedic meaning arises in context(s) of use, so that the 'selection' of encyclopaedic meaning is informed by contextual factors. For example, the word *safe* can have different meanings depending on the particular context of use. *Safe* can mean 'unlikely to cause harm' when used in the context of a child playing with a spade. Alternatively *safe* can mean 'unlikely to come to harm' when used in the context of a beach that has been saved from development as a tourist resort. Fourthly, the encyclopaedic approach views lexical items as points of access to **encyclopaedic knowledge**. Accordingly, words selectively provide access to particular parts of the vast **semantic potential** of encyclopaedic knowledge. Fifthly, while the central meaning associated with a word is relatively stable, the encyclopaedic knowledge that each word provides access to is dynamic. For instance, the knowledge that the **lexical concept** [CAR] provides access to continues to be modified as a result of our ongoing interaction with cars, our acquisition of knowledge regarding cars.

entrenchment The establishment of a **linguistic unit** as a cognitive pattern or routine in the mind of an individual **language user**. The greater the **frequency** of the linguistic unit in the language input the more entrenched the unit is likely to become. Entrenchment is a notion associated in particular with **Cognitive Grammar**. (See also **usage-based model, usage-based thesis**.)

Event space The **mental space** which encodes the time-reference currently in focus in discourse. Normally the event space and the **focus space** coincide. However, sometimes an event space can be built with respect to a focus space and thus can diverge from it. One way in which this happens is due to perfect aspect, which signals that an earlier or later event has relevance at a later or earlier point in time respectively. In this case, the earlier/later event is built in the event space, and the event/time for which structure in the event space has relevance is contained in the focus space. (See also **base space, Mental Spaces Theory, viewpoint space**.)

Event structure metaphor A series of metaphors that often interact in the interpretation of utterances. The individual metaphors that make up the Event Structure Metaphor, together with linguistic examples, are shown in Table 4.

As the individual metaphors in the Event Structure Metaphor work together they thereby comprise a **metaphor system**. They can also be employed by a **specific-level metaphor** exhibiting the phenomenon known as **inheritance**.

excerpting A grammatical operation in which an unbounded mass entity is converted into a countable entity by virtue of a portion of the mass being 'excerpted'. For instance in the following:

1. It is time to spend money
2. It is time to spend some money

the mass noun *money* undergoes an excerpting operation by virtue of the quantifier *some* which serves to excerpt a portion of the unbounded entity money. Excerpting contrasts with the grammatical operation known as **debounding**. (See also **Conceptual Structuring System Approach**.)

exclusionary fallacy According to *Ronald Langacker*, a fallacy in which linguists reason that one analysis or explanation for a given linguistic phenomenon

Table 4. The Event Structure Metaphor

Metaphor:	STATES ARE LOCATIONS (BOUNDED REGIONS IN SPACE)
Example:	*John is in love*
Metaphor:	CHANGE IS MOTION (FROM ONE LOCATION TO ANOTHER)
Example:	*Things went from bad to worse*
Metaphor:	CAUSES ARE FORCES
Example:	*Her argument forced me to change my mind*
Metaphor:	ACTIONS ARE SELF-PROPELLED MOVEMENTS
Example:	*We are moving forward with the new project*
Metaphor:	PURPOSES ARE DESTINATIONS
Example:	*We've finally reached the end of the project*
Metaphor:	MEANS ARE PATHS (TO DESTINATIONS)
Example:	*We completed the project via an unconventional route*
Metaphor:	DIFFICULTIES ARE IMPEDIMENTS TO MOTION
Example:	*It's been uphill all the way on this project*
Metaphor:	EVENTS ARE MOVING OBJECTS
Example:	*Things are going smoothly in the operating theatre*
Metaphor:	LONG-TERM PURPOSEFUL ACTIVITIES ARE JOURNEYS
Example:	*The government is without direction*

necessarily excludes another. One version of the exclusionary fallacy is the **rule/list fallacy.**

experiential basis According to **Conceptual Metaphor Theory,** conceptual metaphors are grounded in the nature of our everyday interaction with the world, either directly as in the case of primary metaphors or indirectly as in the case of compound metaphors. In other words they have an experiential basis. To illustrate, consider the following examples:

1. The price of shares is *going up*
2. She got a *high* score in her exam

These utterances provide linguistic evidence for the **metaphor** QUANTITY IS VERTICAL ELEVATION (also known as MORE IS UP): there is a conventional reading related to QUANTITY. In (1) the sentence refers to an increase in share prices. In (2) it refers to an exam result that represents a numerical quantity. Although each of these readings is perfectly conventional, the lexical items that provide these readings, *going up* and *high*, refer literally to the concept of VERTICAL ELEVATION. Examples like these suggest that QUANTITY and VERTICAL ELEVATION are associated in some way at the conceptual level.

According to *George Lakoff and Mark Johnson*, the architects of Conceptual Metaphor Theory, QUANTITY and VERTICAL ELEVATION are often correlated, and these correlations are ubiquitous in our everyday experience. For instance, when we increase the height of something there is typically more of it. If water is poured into a glass this results in a corresponding increase in both height (vertical elevation) and quantity of water. According to Lakoff and Johnson, this kind of correlation, experienced in our everyday lives, gives rise to the formation of an association at the conceptual level, which is reflected in the linguistic examples. According to this view, conceptual metaphors are always at least partially motivated by and grounded in experience.

experiential domain   see **domain (2)**

external secondary reference object   A kind of **secondary reference object** which serves to furnish the primary reference object with axial properties in order to locate the figure. An external secondary reference object is external to the primary reference object but not encompassing. For instance, in a sentence such as the following: *The church is to the left of the grocery store*, the spatial scene is viewed from a particular location and perspective by a viewer. Here the viewer constitutes an external secondary reference object who imposes particular axial properties on the primary reference object by virtue of projecting his/her own left/right axis on the spatial scene being viewed. (See also encompassing secondary reference object.)

extragrammatical idioms Examples of idiomatic expressions of this kind do not obey the usual rules of grammar. An example from English is: *all of a sudden*. In this expression, the quantifier *all* is followed by a preposition phrase where we would expect to find a noun phrase. Furthermore, an adjective, *sudden*, occurs after a determiner where we might expect to find a noun. Extragrammatical idioms contrast with grammatical idioms. (See also Construction Grammar (1)).

[F]

facet A term coined by *Alan Cruse*. A facet is a word sense that is due to the part-whole structure of an entity and is selected by a specific utterance context. As with a sub-sense, a facet is context-dependent, because the distinctions between facets only arise in certain sentential contexts. For example, consider the lexical item *book*. By virtue of its structure, the concept BOOK consists of both TEXT (the informational content of a book) and TOME (the physical entity consisting of pages and binding). However, these facets only become apparent in certain sentential contexts. This is illustrated below:

1. That book is really heavy
2. That book is really interesting

The example in (1) refers to the TOME facet of *book* while (2) refers to the TEXT facet. It is sentential context (the presence of the expressions *thick* versus *interesting*) rather than context of use that induces a particular facet. (See also **autonomy, contextual modulation, sub-sense.**)

family resemblance A notion in **Prototype Theory** in which a particular member of a category can be assessed as to how well it reflects the **prototype structure** of the category it belongs to. This is achieved based on how many salient attributes belonging to the **prototype** the category member shares. The degree of overlap between shared attributes reflects a category member's degree of family resemblance. For instance, an ostrich cannot fly so lacks a salient attribute associated with the prototype structure of the category BIRD. However, it shares other salient attributes, such as having a beak and wings. Thus it exhibits family resemblance but does not exhibit the same strength of family resemblance as a robin, for instance, which can fly.

fictive motion A term coined by *Leonard Talmy*. The ascription of motion to an entity that cannot undergo veridical motion. For instance, in the following utterance: *The fence runs across the field*, motion is being ascribed to an entity which cannot actually undergo motion. This is an instance of fictive motion.

field-based reference frame A **reference frame** involving a **spatial relation** established between a **figure** and a **reference object** in which the **axial properties** associated with the reference object derive from an **encompassing secondary reference object**. For instance, in the following example: *John is in front of Mary in the queue*, *the queue* serves as an encompassing secondary reference object, providing the primary reference object with an orientational frame. That is, Mary can be turned with her back to John, and yet John is still 'in front' by virtue of the directionality provided by the queue. In other words, the reference object, Mary, is provided with particular axial properties by virtue of being encompassed by the queue. (See also **reference frame, region, spatial relation, spatial scene**.)

figure The most salient element in **figure-ground organisation**. An idea developed in Gestalt psychology and applied in cognitive linguistics in particular by *Leonard Talmy* in his **conceptual structuring system approach**.

figure-ground organisation Human perception appears to automatically segregate any given **spatial scene** into a figure and a ground. A figure is an entity that, among other things, possesses a dominant shape, due to a definite contour or prominent colouring. The figure stands out against the ground, the part of a scene that is relegated to 'background'. In the scene depicted in Figure 14 the figure is the lighthouse and the ground is made up of the grey horizontal lines against which the figure stands out.

　　The phenomenon of figure-ground organisation was pointed out by the Danish psychologist Edgar Rubin

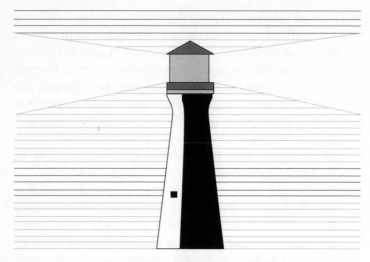

Figure 14. Figure-ground organisation

in 1915. Rubin proposed a number of perceptual differences between the figure and ground. For instance, a figure appears to be thing-like, a contour appears at the edge of the figure's shape, it appears closer to the viewer and in front of the ground, it appears more dominant and is better remembered. In contrast, the ground appears to be substance-like, is relatively formless, appears further away and extends behind the figure, is less dominant, and is less well remembered. Figure-ground organisation has been influential in cognitive linguistics, and has been generalised to language by *Talmy* with his notions of **figure** and **ground,** also known as **reference object,** and by *Langacker* with the theoretical constructs **trajector** and **landmark.**

Talmy has proposed that in linguistic terms, smaller and more mobile objects are typically interpreted as figures, while larger, more immovable objects which serve to locate other objects are typically interpreted as the ground. This observation accounts for the asymmetric behaviour of linguistically encoded spatial scenes. For instance, in the following utterances which are straightforward reversals of one another, while the first utterance is acceptable the second is normally judged as being semantically anomalous as indicated by the question mark.

1. <u>The bike</u> is near [the house]
2. ?[The house] is near <u>the bike</u>

This suggests that the grammatical organisation of linguistically encoded spatial scenes reflects figure-ground organisation. While the subject position corresponds to the figure, the object position corresponds to the ground. The unnaturalness of the second sentence is due to the fact that an entity that would be more likely to serve as the ground in a spatial relation holding between a bike and a house is placed in the position associated with the figure (see also **reference frame, secondary reference object.**)

focal adjustment A notion in **Cognitive Grammar**. Relates to the way in which attention is differentially focused on a particular aspect of a given scene. This is achieved in language by a range of focal adjustments which 'adjust the focus' on a particular aspect of any given scene by using different linguistic expressions or different grammatical constructions to describe that scene. The visual metaphor that the expression 'focal adjustment' rests upon emphasises the fact that visual perception is central to how we focus attention upon aspects of experience. By choosing a particular focal adjustment and thus linguistically 'organising' a scene in a specific way, the speaker imposes a unique **construal** upon that scene. There are three **parameters of focal adjustment** which provide different ways of focusing attention upon and thus construing a scene.

focus input In a **single scope network,** the input space whose structure is the focus of the structuring in the **blended space.** That is, content from the focus input is structured by the **frame** supplied by the **framing input.** (See also **Blending Theory, input spaces, integration network.**)

focus of attention One of the kinds of **pattern** which serve to govern the distribution of attention in the **attentional system.** This pattern is illustrated by the following examples:

1. The wine merchant sold the champagne to Edith
2. Edith bought the champagne from the wine merchant

In the first sentence the seller, *the wine merchant*, is the focus of attention while in the second example the purchaser, *Edith*, is the focus of attention. This results from the mapping of attention onto a particular entity in the scene. The **conceptual structuring system** encodes this in two ways: firstly, by the selection of one of several verbs relating to the COMMERICAL EVENT **frame** (*buy* versus *sell*, for example); and secondly by the associated word order. (See also **Conceptual Structuring System Approach.**)

focus space The **mental space** where new content is currently being added at the moment of speaking. (See also **base space, event space, Mental Spaces Theory, viewpoint space.**)

force-dynamics system One of the **schematic systems** which make up the **conceptual structuring system**. This system relates to our experience of how physical entities interact with respect to force, including the exertion and resistance of force, the blockage of force and the removal of such blockage.

The force-dynamics system assumes two entities that exert force. The agonist is the entity that receives focal attention, and the antagonist is the entity that opposes the agonist, either overcoming the force of the agonist or failing to overcome it. The force intrinsic to the agonist is either 'towards action' or 'towards rest', and the force intrinsic to the antagonist is the opposite. Consider the set of examples below that encode physical entities. The subscripts AGO and ANT represent 'agonist' and 'antagonist', respectively:

1. [the ball]$_{AGO}$ kept rolling because of [the breeze]$_{ANT}$
2. [Isabella]$_{AGO}$ kept standing despite [the gale]$_{ANT}$
3. [the ball]$_{AGO}$ kept rolling despite [the mud]$_{ANT}$
4. [the ball]$_{AGO}$ stayed lying on the slope because of [the grass]$_{ANT}$

In (1), the force tendency of the agonist *the ball* is towards rest, but this is overcome by the greater force of the antagonist *the breeze*, which is towards motion and thus stands in a causal relationship with the agonist. In (2), the force tendency of the agonist *Isabella* is also towards rest, and in this case the agonist's force is greater. In (3), the force tendency of the agonist, *the ball*, is towards motion, and the agonist's force is greater than the opposing force of the antagonist, *the mud*. Finally, in (4), the force tendency of the agonist, *the ball*, is also towards motion, but this time the opposing force of the antagonist, *the grass*, is greater and prevents the motion. In these examples the force dynamics of the interaction are expressed by **closed class forms**: the conjunctions *because of* or *despite*. While *because of* encodes the greater force of the antagonist, which overcomes the force of the agonist and thus entails causality, *despite* encodes the greater force of the agonist. (See also **attentional system, Conceptual Structuring System Approach, configurational system, perspectival system, schematic categories.**)

formal blend Involves **selective projection** of specific lexical forms ('word projection') to the **blended space** in an **integration network**. For instance, the **XYZ construction** involves formal blending, in which the **construction (1)** provides a template which guides the process of formal blending: which sorts of forms can undergo **conceptual integration** and in which order, in order to produce a specific instance of the XYZ construction, for example *Death is the mother of beauty*, in the blended space. (See also **Blending Theory.**)

formal idioms Idioms of this kind provide a syntactic **frame** or template into which different lexical items can be inserted. An example of a formal idiom is the **let alone construction**. The template provided by this construction can be filled with all sorts of lexical items. In other words, this type of idiom is productive. Formal idioms contrast with **substantive idioms**. (See also **Construction Grammar (1), idiomatic expressions.**)

formal linguistics Approaches to modelling language that posit explicit mechanical devices or procedures operating on theoretical **primitives** in order to produce the complete set of linguistic possibilities in a given language. Such mechanical devices are stated in terms of complex formalisms inspired by work in mathematics, computer science and logic. Formal approaches typically take a **modular approach** to language and the mind, and assume that the goal of linguistic enquiry is to capture complex linguistic phenomena in as precise and economical a way as possible. Examples of such approaches include the paradigm of Generative Grammar developed by Noam Chomsky and the tradition known as formal semantics inspired by the work of philsopher of language Richard Montague.

foundation-expansion spaces In **Mental Spaces Theory**, the 'If A then B' **construction (1)** serves as a **space builder** to set up two successive spaces: the foundation space and the expansion space. The foundation space is a hypothetical **mental space** set up by the space builder *if*. The expansion space is set up by the space builder *then*. While the foundation space is hypothetical relative to the **base space,** whatever holds in the foundation space is 'fact' relative to the expansion space and the structure in the expansion space is entailed by it. For instance, in the utterance, *If I won the lottery then I would buy a Rolls-Royce*, the *if* clause builds a space in which I win the lottery. The *then* clause builds a space in which, given this 'fact', I buy a Rolls-Royce.

frame A schematisation of experience (a knowledge structure), which is represented at the conceptual level and held in long-term memory and which relates elements and entities associated with a particular culturally embedded scene, situation or event from human experience. Frames include different sorts of knowledge including attributes, and relations between attributes,

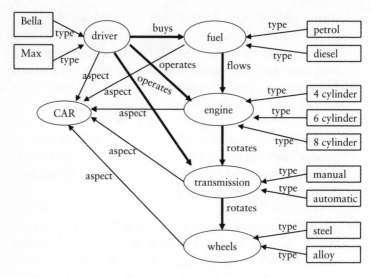

Figure 15. CAR frame

as illustrated by the diagrammatic representation for the frame for CAR in Figure 15.

A frame is related to the notion of a **domain (1)**. Important work on the notion of frames which has been influential in **cognitive linguistics** has been carried out by *Lawrence Barsalou*. (See also **Blending Theory, encyclopaedic semantics, Frame Semantics, semantic frame**.)

frame semantics An approach to **cognitive lexical semantics** developed by *Charles Fillmore*. Attempts to uncover the properties of the structured inventory of knowledge associated with words, and to consider what consequences the properties of this knowledge system might have for a model of semantics. The central construct in Frame Semantics is that of the **semantic frame**. (See also **encyclopaedic knowledge, encyclopaedic semantics, frame**.)

framing input In a **single scope network**, the input space which serves to structure the **blended space** by virtue of projection of its **frame**. (See also **Blending Theory, focus input, input spaces, integration network**.)

frequency A central idea in a **usage-based model** of language. The relative frequency with which a particular word or **construction** is encountered by the speaker is held to affect the nature of the language system. This follows as a **linguistic unit** that is more frequently encountered becomes more entrenched (see **entrenchment**) in the language system. According to this view, the most entrenched linguistic units tend to shape the language system in terms of patterns of use, at the expense of less frequent and thus less well entrenched words or constructions. (See also **usage-based thesis**.)

full-specification model An approach to **cognitive lexical semantics** associated with the work of *George Lakoff*. In his work on the English preposition **over** Lakoff argued for a highly detailed inventory of senses as being stored by the **language user** in semantic memory. This full-specification approach towards **polysemy** has subsequently been criticised, for, among other things, being methodologically unconstrained and for failing to distinguish between lexical concepts that must be stored in the mind of a language user and meanings associated with a word due to context and pragmatic inferencing. (See also **lexical concept, polysemy fallacy, Principled Polysemy**.)

fusion (1) In **Construction Grammar** (2), the process whereby a verb's **participant roles** are integrated with a construction's **argument roles**. The process of fusion is governed by two principles: the **Semantic Coherence Principle** and the **Correspondence Principle**.

fusion (2)   One of the two component processes of **lexical concept integration** in **LCCM Theory**. Fusion, the second compositional process, consists of two further constituent processes which are held to occur in tandem: (1) **integration** and (2) **interpretation**.

fuzzy category   Relates to findings deriving from **Prototype Theory**. A fuzzy category, which can be contrasted with a **classical category**, is a category whose members exhibit degrees of **family resemblance**, with the category borders not being clearly defined. For instance, FURNITURE is a fuzzy category in that while 'table' and 'chair' are clearly members, some people judge artefacts such as 'picture' and 'carpet' as belonging to this category while for others such objects are better thought of as belonging to a related category such as FURNISHINGS. Moreover, context may influence which category we judge entities as belonging to. (See also **Classical Theory**.)

| G |

generalisation commitment   One of two key commitments of the **cognitive linguistics enterprise**. It constitutes a commitment to the characterisation of general principles that are responsible for all aspects of human language. This commitment follows from the assumption central to cognitive linguistics that language reflects general cognitive mechanisms and processes. Hence the generalisation commitment leads cognitive linguists to search for common organising principles across different language 'systems', such as phonology, syntax, semantics and so on. Such common organising principles include conceptual mechanisms like **metaphor, conceptual blending** and phenomena such as **polysemy**. The generalisation commitment stands in direct opposition to the **modular approach** taken in **formal linguistics**. (See also **cognitive commitment**.)

generators A kind of **metonymic ICM**. Members of some categories are 'generated' by a core subset of category members called generators. These generators are judged to be more prototypical than the other category members that they generate and thus stand for the entire category. For example, the natural numbers are represented by the set of integers between zero and nine, which are combined in various ways in order to produce higher natural numbers. For instance, the number 10 combines the integers 1 and 0. Thus, the entire category NATURAL NUMBERS is generated from a small subset of single-digit integers. This is why the numbers 1 to 9 are judged as more prototypical members of the category NATURAL NUMBERS than much larger numbers. (See also **ideals, paragons, salient examples, social stereotypes, typical examples**.)

generic space In an **integration network**, the generic space provides information that is abstract enough to be common to both (or all) the **input spaces**. **Blending Theory** holds that integration networks are, in part, licensed by interlocutors identifying the structure common to the input spaces, thereby licensing **conceptual integration** and thus the formation of a **blended space**. This is achieved by virtue of the generic space; elements in the generic space are mapped onto **counterparts** in each of the input spaces, which motivates the identification of cross-space counterparts in the input spaces.

generic-level metaphor A term coined by *George Lakoff* and *Mark Turner* in their application of **Conceptual Metaphor Theory** to poetic metaphor. Relates to a relatively schematic or abstract level of metaphoric representation which provides structure that can be inherited by **specific-level metaphor**. For instance, the individual metaphors which make up the **Event Structure Metaphor** are generic-level metaphors and are inherited by more specific metaphors via a process known as **inheritance**.

gestalt An organised whole or unit. The central notion in the movement known as **Gestalt psychology**.

Gestalt psychology A movement in psychology which emerged at the end of the nineteenth century, representing a move away from the atomistic outlook that had been prevalent in psychology, particularly in terms of perception research. Gestalt psychology started with the notion of a **gestalt**, and thus postulated that, in terms of perception, the whole is more than the sum of its parts. Gestalt psychology formalised the perceptual mechanisms that facilitate our experience.

Gestalt psychologists such as Max Wertheimer (1880–1943), Wolfgang Köhler (1887–1967) and Kurt Koffka (1886–1941) were interested in the principles that allow unconscious perceptual mechanisms to construct wholes or gestalts out of incomplete perceptual input. For instance, when a smaller object is located in front of a larger one, we perceive the protruding parts of the larger object as part of a larger whole, even though we cannot see the whole because the parts are discontinuous. This is known as the Principle of Continuation. Gestalt principles such as this are held to capture innate structuring mechanisms that constrain perception. Gestalt psychology has been influential in **cognitive linguistics** in that it provides evidence that unconscious mental processes constrain experience. This general position is adopted by cognitive linguists in refuting **objectivist semantics**. (See also **figure-ground organisation**.)

goals of blending In **Blending Theory, conceptual integration** is held to be motivated by an overarching goal and a number of notable sub-goals. The overarching goal and primary motivation for the process of conceptual integration is to achieve human scale. As the creation of a blended space is an imaginative feat that allows us to 'grasp' a relatively complex idea by viewing it in a new way, this can be best achieved by reducing the complexity of ideas captured in **input spaces** to the level of readily understandable human experience. The sub-goals of conceptual integration, which facilitate the overarching goal, include **compression** of diffuse structure in the input spaces, obtaining global insight and strengthening (by compression) of vital relations in the input spaces into an **inner-space relation** in the **blended space**. This thereby provides a narrative, a 'story', which reduces complexity by decreasing the number of distinct elements into a single element in the blended space.

To illustrate, imagine that you are attending a lecture on evolution, and the professor says 'The dinosaurs appeared at 10 pm, and were extinct by quarter past 10. Primates emerged at five minutes to midnight, humans showed up on the stroke of 12.' This represents an attempt to achieve human scale by

Table 5. Goals of blending

Overarching goal of blending
Achieve human scale
Notable sub-goals
Compress what is diffuse
Obtain global insight
Strengthen vital relations
Come up with a story
Go from many to one

blending the vast tracts of evolutionary time with the time period of a 24-hour day. This is achieved by 'compressing' diffuse structure (over 4.6 billion years of evolution) into a more compact, and thus less complex, structure (a 24-hour day). This achieves human scale, because the 24-hour day is perhaps the most salient temporal unit for humans. This conceptual integration achieves global insight by facilitating the comprehension of evolutionary time, since we have no first-hand experience of the vast timescales involved. The goals of blending are summarised in Table 5.

goodness-of-example ratings An experimental means, devised by *Eleanor Rosch* in the early 1970s, to investigate the **prototype structure** of categories. Rosch conducted a series of experiments in which subjects were asked to provide so-called 'goodness-of-example' ratings for between fifty and sixty members of each category, based on the extent to which each member was representative of the category. Typically, subjects were provided with a seven-point scale. They were asked to rate a particular member of the category along this scale, with a rating of 1 indicating that the member is highly representative, and a rating of seven indicating that the entity was not very representative. The experiments Rosch employed in order to obtain goodness-of-example ratings were 'linguistic' experiments. That is, subjects were presented with word lists rather than visual images. Table 6 presents a summary of some of the goodness-of-example ratings uncovered by Rosch for five categories.

governing principles (also **optimality principles**) In **Blending Theory**, the principles that have been proposed in order to constrain the process of **conceptual integration** or blending. These principles operate in a way that facilitates the **goals of blending**. A number of governing principles have been proposed by *Gilles Fauconnier* and *Mark Turner* in their 2002 book *The Way We Think*. These are summarised in Table 7.

graded grammaticality A property associated with the **utterance** (an actual instance of language use). Concerns the observation that utterances occur spontaneously and often exhibit degrees of grammatical well-formedness. Grammatical well-formedness is not a criterial property of an utterance, unlike the related construct of the **sentence**. For example, in terms of structure, an utterance may consist of a single word (*Hi!*), a phrase (*No way!*), an incomplete sentence *(Did you put the . . .?)*, or a sentence that contains errors of pronunciation or grammar because the speaker is tired, distracted or excited, and so on. (See also **graded grammaticality judgements, usage-based thesis.**)

graded grammaticality judgements These arise due to the phenomenon of **graded grammaticality**. Graded grammaticality judgements relate to the observation that

Table 6. Goodness-of-example ratings

Rank	BIRD	FRUIT	VEHICLE	FURNITURE	WEAPON
Top eight (from more to less representative)					
1	Robin	Orange	Automobile	Chair	Gun
2	Sparrow	Apple	Station wagon	Sofa	Pistol
3	Bluejay	Banana	Truck	Couch	Revolver
4	Bluebird	Peach	Car	Table	Machine gun
5	Canary	Pear	Bus	Easy chair	Rifle
6	Blackbird	Apricot	Taxi	Dresser	Switchblade
7	Dove	Tangerine	Jeep	Rocking chair	Knife
8	Lark	Plum	Ambulance	Coffee table	Dagger
9	Swallow	Grapes	Motorcycle	Rocker	Shotgun
10	Parakeet	Nectarine	Streetcar	Love seat	Sword
Bottom ten (from more to less representative)					
10	Duck	Pawpaw	Rocket	Counter	Words
9	Peacock	Coconut	Blimp	Clock	Hand
8	Egret	Avocado	Skates	Drapes	Pipe
7	Chicken	Pumpkin	Camel	Refrigerator	Rope
6	Turkey	Tomato	Feet	Picture	Airplane
5	Ostrich	Nut	Skis	Closet	Foot
4	Titmouse	Gourd	Skateboard	Vase	Car
3	Emu	Olive	Wheelbarrow	Ashtray	Screwdriver
2	Penguin	Pickle	Surfboard	Fan	Glass
1	Bat	Squash	Elevator	Telephone	Shoes

Table 7. Governing principles

Governing principle	Definition
The Topology Principle	Other things being equal, set up the blend and the inputs so that useful topology in the inputs and their outer-space relations is reflected by inner-space relations in the blend. (F&T, 2002: 327)
The Pattern Completion Principle	Other things being equal, complete elements in the blend by using existing integrated patterns as additional inputs. Other things being equal, use a completing frame that has relations that can be compressed versions of the important outer-space vital relations between the inputs. (F&T, 2002: 328)
The Integration Principle	Achieve an integrated blend. (F&T, 2002: 328)
The Maximisation of Vital Relations Principle	Other things being equal, maximize vital relations in the network. In particular, maximize the vital relations in the blended space and reflect them in outer-space vital relations. (F&T, 2002: 330)
The Web Principle	Other things being equal, manipulating the blend as a unit must maintain the web of appropriate connections to the input space easily and without additional surveillance of composition. (F&T, 2002: 331)

Table 7. continued

Governing principle	*Definition*
The Unpacking Principle	Other things being equal, the blend all by itself should prompt for the reconstruction of the entire network. (F&T, 2002: 332)
The Relevance Principle	Other things being equal, an element in the blend should have relevance, including relevance for establishing links to other spaces and for running the blend. Conversely, an outer-space relation between the inputs that is important for the purposes of the network should have a corresponding compression in the blend. (F&T, 2002: 333)

the grammatical 'well-formedness' associated with any given **utterance** is a matter of degree rather than an all-or-nothing affair. For example, the acceptability of passive constructions is determined by a number of factors and is a matter of degree. A question mark before the sentence indicates that the sentence is not perfectly well-formed but is acceptable. Two question marks indicate somewhat less acceptability.

1. This view was enjoyed by Lily and George
2. ?A view was enjoyed by Lily and George
3. ??Views were enjoyed by Lily and George

The examples above become progressively less acceptable as the subject of the sentence moves from being definite or 'individuated' to becoming less definite or individuated. In the examples below, the utterances become progressively less acceptable the less the verb relates to a prototypical physical action.

4. George was tickled by Lily
5. ?George was wanted by Lily
6. ??George was resembled by his brother

grammar-lexicon continuum see **lexicon-grammar continuum**

grammatical idioms These are **idiomatic expressions** that obey the usual rules of grammar. For example, in the grammatical idiom *spill the beans*, a verb takes a noun phrase complement. Grammatical idioms contrast with **extragrammatical idioms**. (See also **Construction Grammar (1)**.)

grammaticalisation (also **grammaticisation**) The process whereby lexical or content words acquire grammatical functions or existing grammatical units acquire further grammatical functions. Grammaticalisation has received a great deal of attention within **cognitive linguistics**. This is because grammaticalisation is characterised by interlaced changes in the form and meaning of a given **construction (1)** and can therefore be seen as a process that is essentially grounded in meaning. Furthermore, cognitive linguists argue that semantic change in grammaticalisation is a function of language use and thus is a usage-based phenomenon. (See also **closed class forms, open class forms, usage-based thesis**.)

grammaticisation see **grammaticalisation**

ground (1) see **reference object**

ground (2) In **Cognitive Grammar**, this term relates to any **utterance** and includes the participants, the time of speaking and the immediate physical context. **Subjective construal** and **objective construal** are understood relative to the notion of ground.

ground-based reference frame The simplest kind of **reference frame**. It involves just a (primary) **reference object** and employs the intrinsic geometry of this reference object in order to locate the figure. For instance, in an utterance such as: *The grocery store is next to the office building*, the office building has an intrinsic front, back and sides to which the speaker appeals in describing the location of the grocery store. Therefore, this type of reference frame is ground- (or reference-object) based.

grounding predication In **Cognitive Grammar**, a grounding predication is a schematic category that relates a particular word class to the **ground**. This is referred to as 'grounding'. For instance, nouns are grounded by determiners and finite clauses are grounded by tense and by modals which link the process designated by the clause to the specific **utterance**.

guidepost-based reference frame Involves an **external secondary reference object** which is typically a non-animate entity and which is external to the primary **reference object**. For instance, in a sentence such as the following: *The bike is the river side of the office block*, *the river*, the external secondary reference object, identifies that portion of *the office block*, the primary reference object, with respect to which the bike is located. (See also **figure**, **figure-ground organisation**, **reference frame**, **region**, **spatial relation**, **spatial scene**.)

guiding principles of cognitive approaches to grammar
The two central assumptions which guide and thereby give rise to **cognitive approaches to grammar**. These are: the **symbolic thesis** and the **usage-based thesis**.

guiding principles of cognitive semantics As with the larger enterprise of **cognitive linguistics** of which it is a part, **cognitive semantics** is not a single unified framework. Those researchers who identify themselves as cognitive semanticists typically have a diverse set of foci and interests. Nevertheless, there are four guiding principles that collectively characterise a cognitive approach to semantics. These are: (1) the thesis of **embodied cognition**; (2) the thesis that **semantic structure reflects conceptual structure**; (3) the thesis that **meaning representation is encyclopaedic**; and (4) the thesis that **meaning construction is conceptualisation**.

H

hiding and highlighting The idea in **Conceptual Metaphor Theory** that when a **target domain** is structured in terms of a particular **source domain**, this highlights certain aspects of the target while simultaneously hiding other aspects. For example, invoking the metaphor ARGUMENT IS WAR highlights the adversarial nature of argument but hides the fact that argument often involves an ordered and organised development of a particular topic (*He won the argument, I couldn't defend that point,* and so on). In contrast, the metaphor AN ARGUMENT IS A JOURNEY highlights the progressive and organisational aspects of arguments while hiding the confrontational aspects (*We'll proceed in step-by-step fashion; We've covered a lot of ground*).

hierarchy of domain complexity A theoretical construct in **Cognitive Grammar**. Concepts presuppose the domains against which they are understood, leading ultimately to domains that do not presuppose anything else. This gives rise to a hierarchy of domain complexity in which a domain lower in the hierarchy is presupposed by the domain(s) higher up. For instance, consider the lexical item *knuckle*. This profiles a concept that is understood with respect to the domain HAND. In turn, the domain HAND is understood with respect to the domain ARM; ARM is understood with respect to the domain BODY, and BODY is understood more generally in terms of (three-dimensional) SPACE. However, it is difficult to envisage another domain in terms of which we understand SPACE. This follows as SPACE is a **basic domain**: one that derives directly from sensory experience of the world, such as visual perception and our experience of motion and touch. Thus SPACE is not understood in terms of a further conceptual domain but is directly grounded in terms of **embodied experience**. This hierarchy of complexity is illustrated in Figure 16. (See also **abstract domain**, **base**, **domain (1)**, **profile**, **scope of predication**.)

highlighting see **hiding and highlighting**

holophrase When a child first produces identifiable units of language at around the age of twelve months these are individual lexical items. Yet, these lexical items do not relate to the corresponding adult form in terms of function. Instead, the child's first words appear to be equivalent to whole phrases and sentences of adult language in terms of communicative intention. For this reason, these early words are known as holophrases. These can have a range of goal-directed communicative

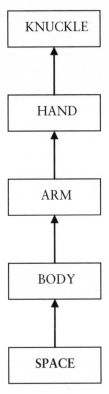

Figure 16. Hierarchy of domain complexity

intentions. For instance, the developmental psycholin-guist *Michael Tomasello* in a study of his daughter's early language acquisition reported a range of uses associated with holophrases, as captured in Table 8.

homologous categories Domains such as TIME and SPACE which appear to share certain structural properties and can thus exhibit **conceptual alternativity**. For instance, both SPACE and TIME can be conceived in terms of quantity. For example, in response to the following

Table 8. Communicative functions of holophrases

Holophrase	Communicative function
Phone	*First use*: in response to hearing the telephone ring
	Second use: to describe activity of 'talking' on the phone
	Third use: to name the phone
	Fourth use: as a request to be picked up in order to talk on the phone
Towel	*First use*: using a towel to clean a spill
	Second use: to name the towel
Make	*First use*: as a request that a structure be built when playing with blocks
Mess	*First use*: to describe the state resulting from knocking down the blocks
	Second use: to indicate the desire to knock down the blocks

question *How far is London from Brighton?* one could answer either *Fifty miles* (SPACE) or *About an hour* (TIME).

homonymy A lexical relation which concerns two or more distinct words that happen to share the same form in sound (homophones) and/or in writing (homographs). For example, the form *bank* relates to two different words with unrelated meanings, 'financial institution' and 'side of a river'. These two senses are not only synchronically unrelated (unrelated in current usage) but also historically unrelated. The word *bank* with the meaning 'side of a river' has been in the English language for much longer, and is related to the Old Icelandic word for 'hill', while the word *bank* meaning 'financial institution' was borrowed from the

Italian *banca*, meaning 'money changer's table'. (See also **monosemy, polysemy.**)

$\boxed{\text{I}}$

ICLA International Cognitive Linguistics Association. The official website of the Association is: www.cognitivelinguistics.org.

ICLC International Cognitive Linguistics Conference. A series of biennial conferences which was inaugurated in 1989 at the University of Duisburg in Germany.

ICM see **idealised cognitive model**

ID Principle see **Access Principle**

Ideal A kind of **metonymic ICM**. An ideal ICM contrasts with **social stereotypes** and **typical examples**. For example, we might have an ideal for the category POLITICIAN: someone who is public-spirited, altruistic, hardworking and so on. This may contrast with our stereotype of politicians as egotistical and power-hungry. **Typicality effects** occur when the ideal stands metonymically for the entire category. For instance, with respect to our ideal the utterance *He's a great politician* might be interpreted as a positive evaluation. However, with respect to our social stereotype, the same utterance would be interpreted as a negative evaluation. (See also **generators, paragons, salient examples.**)

ideal meaning A term coined by *Anette Herskovits* in her work on English prepositions to refer to the central or most salient **lexical concept** associated with a given linguistic unit. (See also **cognitive lexical semantics, over, prototype.**)

idealised cognitive model (also **ICM**) A theoretical construct developed by *George Lakoff* in order to account for the **typicality effects** uncovered by **Prototype Theory**. An ICM is a relatively stable mental representation that represents a 'theory' about some aspect of the world and to which words and other linguistic units can be relativised. In this respect, ICMs are similar to the notion of a **frame**, since both relate to relatively complex knowledge structures. However, while ICMs are rich in detail, they are 'idealised' because they abstract across a range of experiences rather than representing specific instances of a given experience. For instance, the **lexical concept** [BACHELOR] is understood with respect to a MARRIAGE ICM which includes schematic information relating a marriage age, a marriage ceremony, the social, legal, religious and moral dimensions and responsibilities associated with marriage, the participants involved in marriage and the conditions governing their status before and after the event of the marriage ceremony, different events associated with the trajectory of marriage, including the marriage ceremony itself, venues for performing the marriage ceremony, and so forth. According to Lakoff, ICMs are employed in cognitive processes such as categorisation and reasoning. As ICMs constitute coherent bodies of knowledge representation, the way they are structured is organised in various ways. These include being organised by virtue of the **image schema, metaphor** and **metonymy**. ICMs are also employed in order to structure **mental spaces** during on-line meaning construction. This is achieved via a process known as **schema induction**. (See also **cluster model, metonymic ICM.**)

idiomatic expressions Conventional linguistic units which are not predictable simply by knowing the grammar 'rules' and the vocabulary of a language. For this reason, idiomatic expressions are described as 'non-compositional' and have to be learned whole. Idiomatic expressions were studied by *Charles Fillmore and Paul Kay* in the development of **Construction Grammar (1)**. With their colleague Catherine O'Connor they developed a typology of idiomatic expressions. These include: **decoding idioms, encoding idioms, grammatical idioms, extragrammatical idioms, substantive idioms, formal idioms, idioms with pragmatic point** and **idioms without pragmatic point**.

idioms with pragmatic point These **idiomatic expressions** have a very clear pragmatic function, such as greeting (*How do you do?*) or expressing a particular attitude (*What's your car doing in my parking space?*). They contrast with **idioms without pragmatic point**. (See also **Construction Grammar (1)**.)

idioms without pragmatic point Idioms of this kind are pragmatically neutral, in the sense that they can be used in any pragmatic context. Expressions like *by and large* and *on the whole* fall into this category. **Idiomatic expressions** of this kind contrast with **idioms with pragmatic point**. (See also **Construction Grammar (1)**.)

image metaphor A kind of **resemblance-based metaphor**. An image metaphor is based on perceived physical resemblance. Metaphors of this kind have been studied in detail by *George Lakoff* and *Mark Turner* and are extremely common in literary language. For instance, in the following utterance: *The supermodel is just a* *twig*, a perceived resemblance is being established between the supermodel and the twig. The professional success of a supermodel dictates that she be tall and thin and thus may appear quite bony. The image metaphor draws our attention to the perceived physical resemblance between a twig and the supermodel.

image schema A relatively abstract conceptual representation that arises directly from our everyday interaction with and observation of the world around us. Image schemas derive from sensory and perceptual experience. Accordingly, they derive from **embodied experience**. For example, gravity ensures that unsupported objects fall to the ground; given the asymmetry of the human vertical axis, we have to stoop to pick up fallen objects, look in one direction (downwards) for fallen objects, and in another (upwards) for rising objects. In other words, our physiology ensures that our vertical axis, which interacts with gravity, gives rise to meaning as a result of how we interact with our environment. According to *Mark Johnson*, the key proponent of the notion of the image schema, this aspect of our experience gives rise to the UP-DOWN image schema. In addition, and as shown by the developmental psychologist *Jean Mandler*, image schemas are emergent. That is because image schemas are functions of our bodies and of our interaction in the world, image schemas arise in conjunction with our physical and psychological development during early childhood via a process termed **perceptual meaning analysis**.

The term 'image' in 'image schema' is equivalent to the use of this term in psychology, where 'imagistic' experience relates to and derives from our experience of the external world. Another term for this type of experience is **sensory experience**. The term 'schema' in 'image schema' means that image schemas are not rich or detailed concepts, but rather are abstract concepts consisting of patterns emerging from repeated instances of embodied experience. Image schemas provide the basis for more richly detailed **lexical concept**s. For example, the CONTAINER image schema consists of the structural elements interior, boundary and exterior: these are the minimum requirements for a CONTAINER. Part of the meaning of the lexical concepts associated with the following forms: *full*, *empty*, *in*, *out*, etc., has to do with the CONTAINER schema.

It has also been claimed by *George Lakoff* and *Mark Johnson* in their work on **metaphor** that image schemas provide the basis for abstract thought by virtue of serving as the **source domain** in metaphoric **mappings**. The importance of image schemas is that they are held to provide the concrete basis for these metaphoric mappings. Consider the image schema PHYSICAL OBJECT. This image schema is based on our everyday interaction with concrete objects like desks, chairs, tables, cars and so on. The image schema is a schematic representation emerging from embodied experience, which generalises over what is common to objects: for example, that they have physical attributes such as colour, weight, shape and so forth. This image schema can be 'mapped onto' an abstract entity like 'inflation', which lacks these physical properties. The consequence of this metaphoric mapping is that we now understand an abstract entity like 'inflation' in terms of a physical object. This is illustrated by examples such as the following: *Inflation is giving the government a headache; Inflation makes me sick*. A partial list of those image schemas which have been identified so far is given in Table 9. (See also **image schema transformation**.)

Table 9. A listing of image schemas

SPACE	UP-DOWN, FRONT-BACK, LEFT-RIGHT, NEAR-FAR, CENTRE-PERIPHERY, CONTACT, STRAIGHT, VERTICALITY
CONTAINMENT	CONTAINER, IN-OUT, SURFACE, FULL-EMPTY, CONTENT
LOCOMOTION	MOMENTUM, SOURCE-PATH-GOAL
BALANCE	AXIS BALANCE, TWIN-PAN BALANCE, POINT BALANCE, EQUILIBRIUM
FORCE	COMPULSION, BLOCKAGE, COUNTERFORCE, DIVERSION, REMOVAL OF RESTRAINT, ENABLEMENT, ATTRACTION, RESISTANCE
UNITY/ ITERATION,	MERGING, COLLECTION, SPLITTING,
MULTIPLICITY	PART-WHOLE, COUNT-MASS, LINK(AGE)
IDENTITY	MATCHING, SUPERIMPOSITION
EXISTENCE	REMOVAL, BOUNDED SPACE, CYCLE, OBJECT, PROCESS

image schema transformation Because an **image schema** arises from **embodied experience**, which is ongoing, image schemas can undergo transformations from one image schema into another. For instance, the SOURCE-PATH-GOAL image schema in fact represents such a transformation, which reflects the typical trajectory of locomotion undertaken by an animate entity as shown diagrammatically in Figure 17.

In his work on the English preposition **over**, *George Lakoff* argues that new senses of *over* arise due to image schema transformations. For instance, while *over* has, according to Lakoff, an 'above-across' sense (or **lexical concept**) associated with it, as evidenced by examples such as the following: *John walked over the*

SOURCE   PATH   GOAL

Figure 17. SOURCE-PATH-GOAL image schema

hill, in an example of the following kind: *John lives over the hill*, the focus has switched to the goal, the end point of a motion trajectory. This switch in focus is possible due to image-schema transformation, resulting in a distinct 'end-point focus' sense.

implicit closed class forms Closed class forms that have no phonetic realisation but represent speaker knowledge of grammatical categories such as noun and verb, their sub-categories (for example, count noun and mass noun) and grammatical functions (also known as 'grammatical relations') such as subject and object. Implicit closed class forms contrast with **overt closed class forms**.

inheritance (1) The phenomenon whereby a more **specific-level metaphor** inherits structure from a more **generic-level metaphor**. For instance, a **metaphor** such as LIFE IS A JOURNEY inherits structure from the individual metaphors that make up the **Event Structure Metaphor**. This is illustrated by the examples below:

1. STATES ARE LOCATIONS
   He's *at a crossroads* in his life
2. CHANGE IS MOTION
   He went *from* his forties *to* his fifties without a hint of a mid-life crisis
3. CAUSES ARE FORCES
   He *got a head start* in life

4. PURPOSES ARE DESTINATIONS
   I can't ever seem to *get to where I want to be* in life
5. MEANS ARE PATHS
   He followed *an unconventional course* during his life
6. DIFFICULTIES ARE IMPEDIMENTS TO MOTION
   Throughout his working life problematic professional relationships had somehow always *got in his way*
7. PURPOSEFUL ACTIVITIES ARE JOURNEYS
   His life had been *a rather strange journey*

The target domain for this metaphor is LIFE, while the source domain is JOURNEY. The EVENTS that comprise this metaphor are life events, while the PURPOSES are life goals. However, because this metaphor is structured by the Event Structure Metaphor, LIFE IS A JOURNEY turns out to be a **compound metaphor** that represents a composite mapping drawing from a range of related and mutually coherent metaphors: each of the examples in (1–7) inherits structure from a specific metaphor within the Event Structure Metaphor. (See also **Conceptual Metaphor Theory**.)

inheritance (2)   The idea that constructions in the **contructicon** follow the **Principle of Maximised Motivation** by inheriting structure (form and/or meaning) from one another. This is modelled in **Construction Grammar (2)** by positing a range of **inheritance links** between constructions. (See also **construction (1)**.)

inheritance links   In **Construction Grammar (2)**, the links between constructions in the **constructicon**, allowing one construction to 'inherit' structure from another. The types of inheritance links proposed are: **polysemy**

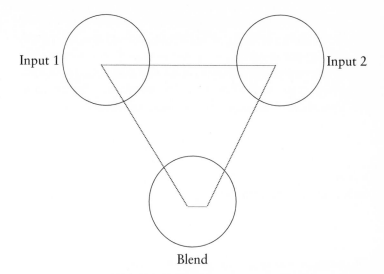

Figure 18. Compression of an outer-space relation

links, **subpart links**, **instance links** and **metaphorical extension links**. Inheritance links serve to instantiate the **Principle of Maximised Motivation**. (See also **construction (1)**, **inheritance**.)

inner-space relation. In an **integration network**, an inner-space relation is a **vital relation** that has undergone **compression** giving rise to **emergent structure** in the **blended space**. Typically, an inner-space relation results from **compression** of an **outer-space relation**, as illustrated by Figure 18.

To illustrate compression of an outer-space relation into an inner-space relation consider the Clinton as French President integration network, as prompted for by the following utterance: *In France, Clinton wouldn't have been harmed by his affair with Monica Lewinsky*, and as discussed in detail in the entry for **conceptual integration**. In this network, we have Bill Clinton, the former American President, in one input space, and the role of French President in the other. One function of the network is to integrate the value Bill Clinton with the role French President. The outer-space vital relation ROLE-VALUE results in an inner-space relation of UNIQUENESS, in which Bill Clinton *is* the French President. (See also **Blending Theory**.)

innovation The process in which an **utterance** provides a meaning or utilises a form that breaks with the **conventions** of the language. This is achieved by virtue of **altered replication**. (See also **normal replication, replicator, Utterance Selection Theory**.)

input spaces An **integration network** possesses two or more input spaces from which structure is projected to the **blended space**. Each input space is a **mental space** structured with respect to the principles developed in **Mental Spaces Theory**. (See also **Blending Theory, generic space**.)

instance A more specific variant of a given **schema**. Instances of schemas serve to **sanction** particular **instantiations**. The relationship between a schema and the more specific schemas which make up its instances are provided in Figure 19.

In Figure 19 the more abstract schema [P [NP]] has a number of more specific schemas related to it: [to me], [on the floor] and [in the garage]. These instances, like the more general schema, are entrenched and thus constitute part of the **language user**'s mental grammar. These are stored together with the more abstract schema as a structured network of

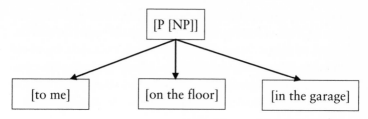

Figure 19. Schema-instance relations

schemas. The relationship between a schema and its instances is known as **schema-instance organisation.** (See also **Cognitive Grammar, usage-based model.**)

instance links One of a number of **inheritance links** between constructions posited in **Construction Grammar (2).** Involves a type of **inheritance (2)** in which one construction is a special case of a related construction. This type of link accounts for the existence of **substantive idioms** in which a particular lexical item or items is/are required for the idiomatic reading to be available. For instance, the following utterance is related to the **resultative construction** by an instance link, where *drive* is required in order to obtain the reading of annoy/make someone mad: *James drove Jenny round the bend.* (See also **construction (1), idiomatic expression.**)

instantiation Specific instances of language use, in which a usage pattern instantiates its corresponding **schema.** Instantiations, therefore, are specific instances of use, arising from a schematic representation. The view that mental schemas license or **sanction** particular instances of use is due to the **usage-based thesis** widely adopted in **cognitive linguistics.** (See also **Cognitive Grammar, usage-based model.**)

integration One of the constituent processes of **fusion (2)** in **LCCM Theory**. Integration involves the construction of larger lexical entities which proceeds by combining linguistic knowledge units: lexical concepts. These larger lexical units, which are termed 'lexical conceptual units', are then subject to **interpretation**. (See also **lexical concept**.)

integration network A structure employed in **Blending theory** in order to model the way in which a **blended space** is achieved. An integration network consists of mental spaces of three kinds: a **generic space**, at least two **input spaces** and a **blended space**. The purpose of the integration network is to facilitate **conceptual integration** of existing **conceptual structure** from different mental spaces and background frames in order to produce **emergent structure**. The basic integration network consists of four mental spaces, as illustrated in Figure 20.

　　The generic space motivates a **matching** operation (represented by the bold lines) in which **counterparts** are identified in the two input spaces. **Selective projection** then serves to project structure from the two input spaces to the blended space.

　　Four kinds of integration network have been identified based on the relative contribution of the input spaces and generic space with respect to the emergent structure of the blended space. These constitute the **simplex network**, the **single scope network**, the **mirror network** and the **double scope network**. (See also **compression, constitutive processes, goals of blending, governing principles, vital relations**.)

intention-reading ability According to *Michael Tomasello*, one of two abilities essential to the uniquely human

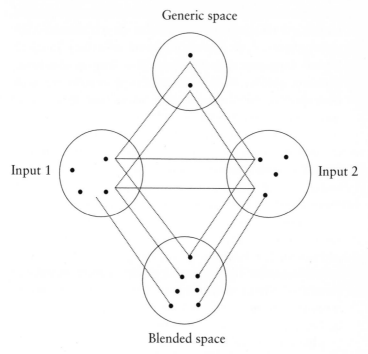

Figure 20. An integration network

ability to acquire language. While the **pattern-finding ability** allows pre-linguistic infants to begin to identify one **linguistic unit** from another, the use of these units requires intention-reading skills, which transform linguistic stimuli from statistical patterns of sound into fully fledged linguistic symbols. In other words, this stage involves 'connecting' the meaning to the form, which gives rise to the form-meaning pairing that make up our knowledge of language. Only then can these linguistic sounds be used for communication. This process takes place when, at around a year old, infants begin to understand that the people around them are 'intentional agents': their actions are deliberate and the actions and states of others can be influenced. The emergence of this understanding allows infants to 'read' the intentions of others. The human intention-reading ability, as it manifests itself in first language acquisition, consists of three specific but interrelated phenomena: **joint attention frames,** the understanding of **communicative intentions** and **role reversal imitation.** (See also **emergentism, socio-cognitive mechanisms in language acquisition.**)

interpretation   The second of the two constituent processes of **fusion (2)** in **LCCM Theory. Interpretation** involves **activation** of part of the **cognitive model profile** to which each selected **lexical concept** in any **utterance** affords **access.** Each lexical concept is interpreted in a way that is in keeping with the larger lexical unit which results from **integration.** That is, those parts of the cognitive model profiles (**semantic potential**) associated with each lexical concept in the larger unit is interpreted in a way that is in keeping with the larger unit. Put another way, integration provides (linguistic) instructions which serve to determine how the various lexical concepts are collectively interpreted and thus the **access route** that each individual lexical concept affords through its **cognitive model profile.** The result is that any given word will provide a unique activation of part of its meaning potential on every occasion of use. This follows as every utterance and thus the resulting **conception** is unique. For instance, the interpretation of *France* in each of the examples below is slightly distinct due to the other lexical concepts it is combined with in each **utterance.** In the first, *France* is interpreted as relating to a geographical landmass, while in the second it is interpreted as relating to citizens of France who voted in a particular way in a particular referendum:

1. France is a country of contrasting landscapes
2. France rejected the EU constitution

Introspective experience see **subjective experience**

Invariance Hypothesis see **Invariance Principle**

Invariance Principle (also **Invariance Hypothesis**) The principle which captures the constraints that govern **cross-domain mappings** in **Conceptual Metaphor Theory**. There are two sorts of constraints that the Invariance Principle captures. Firstly, it stipulates which sorts of source domains can serve particular target domains for a particular conceptual **metaphor**. Secondly, it stipulates the constraints on **metaphorical entailments** that can apply to particular target domains. The Invariance Principle does this by stipulating that in a metaphoric cross-domain mapping, the cognitive topology (the **conceptual structure**) associated with the **source domain** is preserved, or remains invariant, in the mapping operation. However, there is a further stipulation that what is mapped from the source domain must remain consistent with the cognitive topology of the **target domain**.

To illustrate how the Invariance Principle works, consider the concept of DEATH. This can be metaphorically personified in a number of ways (which means that a concept has human-like properties attributed to it such as intentionality and volition). However, the human-like qualities that can be associated with DEATH are restricted: DEATH can 'devour', 'destroy' or 'reap', but death is never metaphorically structured in terms of, for instance, knitting, filling a bath with water or sitting in a rocking chair. What the Invariance Principle does is guarantee that the structure of the source domain must be preserved by the metaphoric mappings in a way consistent with the target domain. This constrains potentially incompatible mappings. As death involves an event of (often sudden) non-existence, only source domains that have an event structure compatible with this can be successfully mapped onto the domain of DEATH. As events such as filling a bath, or sitting in a rocking chair have the 'wrong' sort of event structure, the Invariance Principle predicts that they cannot be employed as source domains for metaphorically conceptualising the domain of DEATH.

Nevertheless, not all cross-domain mappings can be predicted by the Invariance Principle. A further constraint is required in order to account for these exceptions. This is known as the **target domain override** constraint.

Invited Inferencing Theory A theory of semantic change proposed by *Elizabeth Closs Traugott* in order to address regularities in semantic change resulting in **grammaticalisation**. This theory is called the Invited Inferencing Theory of Semantic Change because its main claim is that the form-meaning reanalysis that characterises grammaticalisation arises as a result of situated language use. In other words, this approach assumes that semantic change is usage-based in nature. Traugott argues that pragmatic meaning or inferences that arise in specific contexts come to be reanalysed as part of the conventional meaning associated with a given **construction** (1). Inferences of this kind are invited, in the sense that they are suggested by the context. (See also **pragmatic strengthening**.)

J

joint attention frame The common ground that facilitates understanding of a **communicative intention**, established as a consequence of a particular goal-directed activity. When an infant and an adult are both looking at and playing with a toy, for example, the attention frame consists of the infant, the adult and the toy. While other elements that participate in the scene are still perceived (such as the child's clothes or other objects in the vicinity), it is this 'triadic relationship' between child, adult and toy that is the joint focus of attention. The joint attention frame is one of the elements central to the pre-linguistic infant's developing **intention-reading ability** and is an important idea in *Michael Tomasello*'s account of first language acquisition. (See also **pattern-finding ability, role reversal imitation, socio-cognitive mechanisms in language acquisition**.)

L

landmark (also **LM**) The secondary participant in a **profiled relationship**. (See also **secondary landmark, trajector-landmark organisation**.)

language user A member of a particular linguistic community who, in speaking (and, indeed, in signing or writing), attempts to achieve a particular interactional goal or set of goals using particular linguistic and non-linguistic strategies. Interactional goals include attempts to elicit information or action on the part of the hearer, to provide information, to establish interpersonal rapport (for instance, when 'passing the time of day'), and so on. The linguistic strategies employed to achieve these goals might include the use of speech acts (requesting, informing, promising, thanking and so on), choices over words and grammatical constructions, intonation structures, choices over conforming or not conforming to discourse conventions like turn-taking and so on. Non-linguistic strategies include facial expressions, gesture, orientation of the speaker, proximity of interlocutors in terms of interpersonal space and so on. (See also **conventions, usage-based thesis, utterance, Utterance Selection Theory.**)

LCCM Theory A theory of lexical representation and semantic composition developed by *Vyvyan Evans* that adheres to the **guiding principles of cognitive semantics** and the **guiding principles of cognitive approaches to grammar.** The theory takes its name from the two central constructs upon which the theory is built: the notion of the **lexical concept** and the **cognitive model.** The theory is, in part, a development of and extension of the theory of **Principled Polysemy.**

The central insight of LCCM Theory is that there is a basic distinction between lexical concepts and meaning. While lexical concepts constitute the semantic units conventionally associated with linguistic forms and form an integral part of a **language user**'s individual mental grammar, meaning is a property of situated usage-events (an **utterance**) rather than individual words or linguistic units. Thus meaning is treated not as a function of language per se, but arises from language use. Thus this approach represents a **usage-based model** of language. LCCM Theory develops an account of the nature of lexical concepts and the **encyclopaedic knowledge** that lexical concepts provide **access** to, and of the mechanisms of **lexical concept integration: lexical concept selection** and

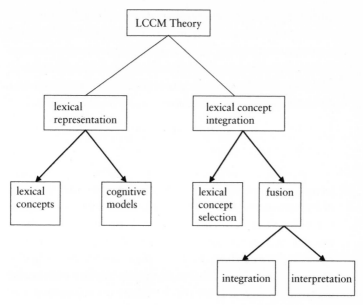

Figure 21. An overview of the architecture of LCCM Theory

fusion (2), which facilitate how lexical concepts are integrated in order to serve as prompts for processes of **conceptualisation**. A diagrammatic representation of the architecture for LCCM Theory is presented in Figure 21.

let alone construction A **formal idiom** studied by *Charles Fillmore, Paul Kay* and Catherine O'Connor in support of their theory of **Construction Grammar (1)**. The *let alone* construction can be described in terms of its syntactic, semantic and pragmatic properties, some of which are regular and some of which are idiosyncratic. The *let alone* construction displays regular syntactic properties and is characterised by the presence of the coordinating conjunction *let alone*, which coordinates two prosodically prominent (stressed) expressions. This construction is illustrated by the sentence in (1) below. In this example, the expressions *basic arithmetic* and *advanced algebra* (labelled as A and B respectively) are prosodically prominent, and are coordinated by *let alone*.

1. John doesn't understand basic arithmetic let alone
   advanced algebra   A
            B

In semantic terms, the construction has the idiosyncratic property that the coordinated expressions are interpreted as contrasted points on a scale, where the second conjunct (*advanced algebra*) has greater emphatic force than the first (*basic arithmetic*). In the context of asking about John's grasp of advanced algebra, as a result of the *let alone construction*, the utterance in (1) conveys the information that because John doesn't understand basic arithmetic, he is even less likely to comprehend advanced algebra. This rests upon the assumption that understanding basic arithmetic is a prerequisite for understanding advanced algebra.

The *let alone* construction also has pragmatic point. Not only does the construction reject a particular proposition (for example, that John understands advanced algebra), but it does so by providing additional relevant information. The relevant information relates to the first conjunct (A), and establishes an implicational scale between the expressions conjoined by *let alone*. If John doesn't understand (A) this implies that he doesn't understand (B). The pragmatic impact of this construction is that by first rejecting a weaker proposition, the proposition that our attention is focused upon (e.g. whether John understands advanced algebra) is more forcefully negated than it would otherwise have been.

level C In **Mental Spaces Theory,** the level at which meaning-construction, or **conceptualisation,** occurs. Level C is a level of conceptual processing 'above' the level of **semantic structure** as encoded by language. Thus meaning-construction is fundamentally conceptual and hence non-linguistic in nature.

level of attention One of the kinds of **pattern** which serve to govern the distribution of attention in the **attentional system.** The 'level of attention' pattern involves the level of detail at which attention is being focused with respect to a particular participant, participants or event. For instance, in the first example below the **focus of attention** is upon the group of friends as a whole. The second example focuses on the internal structure or 'componentiality' of the group. Both examples thus illustrate a different level of attention.

1. the group of friends
2. the friends in the group

(See also **conceptual structuring system, Conceptual Structuring System Approach.**)

lexical concept A unit of **semantic structure** conventionally associated with a linguistic form central to **LCCM Theory.** Together, a lexical concept and a form make up a **linguistic unit**: a conventional form-meaning pairing. Lexical concepts constitute linguistically encoded concepts – that is conceptual knowledge encoded in a form that can be externalised via language. Lexical concepts are conventionally associated with linguistic forms of all kinds including words, bound morphemes, **idiomatic expressions** and grammatical constructions. Accordingly, lexical concepts, by definition, concern purely linguistic knowledge, although a given lexical concept provides **access** to a **cognitive model profile** and thus serves as an **access site** to **encyclopaedic knowledge** which is deployed in the service of building a **conception**. There are a number of properties associated with lexical concepts, perhaps the most important of which is that each lexical concept has a unique **lexical profile**. Examples of four distinct lexical concepts encoded by the form *fly* are illustrated by the examples below. Lexical concepts are glossed by small capitals in square brackets.

1. The plane/bird is flying (in the sky) — [SELF-PROPELLED AERODYNAMIC MOTION]
2. The pilot is flying the plane (in the sky) — [OPERATION OF ENTITY CAPABLE OF AERODYNAMIC MOTION]
3. The child is flying the kite (in the breeze) — [CONTROL OF LIGHT WEIGHT ENTITY]
4. The flag is flying (in the breeze) — [SUSPENSION OF LIGHT WEIGHT OBJECT]

(See also **cognitive model**.)

lexical concept integration In LCCM Theory, the process whereby lexical concepts are integrated in the service of meaning-construction. Lexical concept integration involves two component processes: **lexical concept selection** and **fusion (2)**. (See also **lexical concept**.)

lexical concept selection One of the two component processes of **lexical concept integration**. Lexical concept selection involves selecting the most appropriate **lexical concept** associated with each form in an **utterance**, guided by linguistic and extra-linguistic context. For instance, in the following example: *She approached the bar*, the extra-linguistic context determines whether 'public house bar' or 'court of law bar' are selected. (See also **fusion (2)**.)

lexical profile The defining property of any given **lexical concept**, as each lexical concept has a unique lexical profile. A lexical profile relates to the range of semantic arguments and grammatical constructions with which a given lexical concept conventionally co-occurs and which forms part of the mental knowledge associated with a given lexical concept. The lexical profile thus serves as a principled means of distinguishing lexical concepts conventionally associated with the same form. Two sorts of information form a lexical concept's lexical profile. The first relates to semantic selectional tendencies: the semantic arguments with which a given lexical concept can collocate. The second relates to formal or grammatical selectional tendencies: the formal patterns in which a given lexical concept occurs.

By way of illustration consider the following examples of *fly*. Lexical concepts are glossed by small capitals in square brackets.

1. The plane/bird is flying (in the sky)   [SELF-PROPELLED AERODYNAMIC MOTION]

2. The pilot is flying the plane (in the sky)   [OPERATION OF ENTITY CAPABLE OF AERODYNAMIC MOTION]

3. The child is flying the kite   [CONTROL OF
   (in the breeze)   LIGHTWEIGHT
                                   ENTITY]

4. The flag is flying   [SUSPENSION OF
   (in the breeze)   LIGHTWEIGHT
                                  OBJECT]

Unlike nouns, for which a salient grammatical feature is how they are determined, a salient grammatical feature for verbs is transitivity. In terms of formal dependencies then, the hallmark of the lexical concepts which license the uses of *fly* in (1) and (4) is the lack of a direct object (an intransitive verb). This contrasts with the lexical concepts which sanction the examples in (2) and (3) which both require a direct object (a transitive verb). This distinction in transitivity fails to distinguish (1) from (4) and (2) from (3). For this we must rely on semantic tendencies. The hallmark of each of these lexical concepts is that they require distinct semantic arguments.

For instance, the [SELF-PROPELLED AERODYNAMIC MOTION] lexical concept which is held to sanction the use of *fly* in (1) only applies to entities that are capable of self-propelled aerodynamic motion. Entities that are not self-propelled, such as tennis balls, cannot be used in this sense (*the tennis ball is flying in the sky*).

The lexical concept which underlies the use of *fly* in (2): [OPERATION OF ENTITY CAPABLE OF AERODYNAMIC MOTION], is restricted to the operation by an entity which can be construed as an agent, and moreover to entities that can undergo self-propelled aerodynamic motion. Further, the entity must be able to accommodate the agent and thereby serve as a means of transport. This explains why planes and hot air balloons are compatible with this sense, but entities unable to accommodate an agent are not.

In the case of [CONTROL OF LIGHTWEIGHT ENTITY] as evidenced by the use of *fly* in (3), this lexical concept appears to be restricted to entities that are capable of becoming airborne by turbulence and can be controlled by an agent on the ground. This lexical concept appears to be specialised for objects like kites and model/remote controlled aeroplanes.

The final lexical concept, glossed as [SUSPENSION OF LIGHTWEIGHT OBJECT], selects for entities that can be supported by virtue of air turbulence but remain 'connected to' the ground. This lexical concept applies to flags as well as hair and scarves, which can 'fly' in the wind.

lexicon-grammar continuum The idea that while there is a qualitative distinction between linguistic units encoded by **open class forms** and **closed class forms** respectively, there is not a principled distinction between the two. In other words, in cognitive linguistics it is assumed that 'lexical' and 'grammatical' units are both inherently meaningful, a consequence of the **symbolic thesis**. From this perspective, there is no principled distinction between a mental lexicon and a syntax component. Rather, lexical items and grammatical elements are conceived as forming a continuum. (See also **content meaning**, **linguistic unit**, **schematic meaning**.)

lingueme An element of language that is realised in an **utterance** and that can therefore count as a **replicator**. A lingueme includes sound segments, words, morphemes and grammatical constructions. Crucially, just as each utterance is a unique usage event, so each lingueme is also unique. (See also **Utterance Selection Theory**.)

linguistic relativity (also **Principle of Linguistic Relativity, Sapir-Whorf hypothesis**) The view that the language one speaks affects or determines how you see the world, most famously expounded in the writings of Benjamin Lee Whorf in the 1930s and 1940s, but also influenced by the work of Whorf's teacher, Edward Sapir. The so-called 'strong' version of the principle of linguistic relativity holds that non-linguistic thought is constrained by the categories made available by the language one speaks. The 'weak version' suggests that the language one speaks may influence non-linguistic thought. In recent years evidence has begun to amass supporting the 'weak' version. Cognitive linguistics is compatible with a 'weak' version of the linguistic relativity principle known as 'neo-Whorfianism' most famously expounded by *John Lucy*.

linguistic unit (also **symbolic unit**) A general term for the fundamental unit of language. This term is sometimes employed in cognitive linguistics in place of theory-specific terms such as **symbolic assembly** and **construction (1)**. Cognitive linguists hold that a linguistic unit consists of a conventional pairing of a semantic unit and a form unit, pairing meaning with form. Linguistic units include so-called inflectional morphemes such as the plural marker '-s' as in *toys*, meaningful parts of words such as '-er' in *teacher*, words such as *cat*, complex words such as *cats* made up of 'cat' and '-s', idioms such as *He kicked the bucket*, and sentence level grammatical constructions such as the ditransitive construction, with the schematic meaning X CAUSED Y TO RECEIVE Z, and the form SUBJECT VERB

OBJECT1 OBJECT2 as exemplified by the sentence *John gave Mary a bouquet of flowers*.

location One of the four **schematic categories** in the **perspectival system**. This category relates to the location that a perspective point occupies relative to a given **utterance**. The linguistic system of deixis, for example, works by signalling perspective relative to the speaker's location, and deictic expressions are then interpreted with respect to that point of reference. For instance, in the following examples the perspective point from which the scene is described is different. In (1), the perspective point is located inside the room, while in (2) the perspective point is located outside the room.

1. The door slowly opened and two men walked in
2. Two men slowly opened the door and walked in

This distinction in perspective point is achieved by **closed class forms**. In (1), the subject of the sentence is *the door*, which is the THEME: a passive entity whose location or state is described. In this example, *open* is an intransitive verb: it requires no object. In example (2), the subject of the sentence is *two men*, which is the AGENT: the entity that intentionally performs the action of opening the door. In this example, *open* is transitive (it requires an object: *the door*). What comes first in the sentence (the subject) corresponds to what is viewed first by the human experiencer, and this provides us with clues for reconstructing the perspective point. In (1), as the initiator(s) of the action are not mentioned, we deduce that the initiators of the action are not visible. From this we conclude that the perspective point must be inside the room. In (2) the initiators of the event are mentioned first, so we deduce that the perspective point is exterior to the room. (See also **conceptual system, direction, distance, mode.**)

M

Many Space Model see **Blending Theory**

mapping One of the factors which governs the **attentional system** in the **conceptual structuring system**. Mapping governs the way in which parts of an attention **pattern** are mapped onto parts of the scene described by a linguistic utterance. (See also **Conceptual Structuring System Approach.**)

mappings Correspondences between entities inhering in regions of the **conceptual system**. Some mappings are relatively stable and persist in long-term memory while others are temporary associations set up due to dynamic processes of meaning-construction. Mappings which hold in long-term memory are most commonly associated with **Conceptual Metaphor Theory** and are known as **cross-domain mappings**. Mappings which are more temporary in nature and serve to associate two regions of conceptual space for the purposes of situated understanding are most commonly associated with processes of **conceptual projection** dealt with in **Mental Spaces Theory**.

matching In **Blending Theory**, the operation whereby **counterparts** in **input spaces** are identified by virtue of structure in a **generic space**. (See also **blended space, conceptual integration, integration network.**)

material anchor A physical artefact which both represents and serves as a physical reminder/symbol of a particular

integration network. A material anchor can also be employed in order to prompt for the (re-)construction of a given integration network. Rituals, for instance, often employ material anchors. In the case of Holy Communion, a ritual in various Christian denominations, the bread and the wine that are consumed by worshippers are material anchors which both embody and facilitate the conceptual integration (the union between the human and the divine). Similarly, the wedding ring in the western marriage ritual is a material anchor. The ring both embodies the conceptual integration, representing an unbroken link, and also has a performative function as part of a ritual: the act of placing the ring (which embodies an unbroken link) on the betrothed's finger serves, in part, to join two individuals in matrimony. (See also **Blending Theory**.)

meaning-construction is conceptualisation The fourth of the **guiding principles of cognitive semantics**. Asserts that language itself does not encode meaning. Instead, words (and other linguistic units) are treated as 'prompts' for the construction of meaning. Accordingly, meaning is constructed at the conceptual level (or **level C**). Meaning-construction is equated with **conceptualisation**, a process whereby linguistic units serve as prompts for an array of conceptual operations and the recruitment of background knowledge. On this view, meaning is a process rather than a discrete 'thing' that can be 'packaged' by language. (See also **cognitive semantics**.)

meaning potential A term coined by *Jens Allwood*. Relates to the notion that word-meaning is a function of **encyclopaedic knowledge** plus knowledge of the way the word has been used in the past. On this view, words do not have fixed meanings but only a potential for activation based on interpretation in context.

meaning representation is encyclopaedic The third of the **guiding principles of cognitive semantics**. Holds that **semantic structure** is encyclopaedic in nature. This means that a **lexical concept** does not represent a neatly packaged bundle of meaning (the so-called 'dictionary view'). Rather, lexical concepts serve as **access sites** to vast repositories of knowledge relating to a particular **concept**, conceptual **domain** (1) or **cognitive model**. (See also **cognitive semantics, encyclopaedic semantics, LCCM Theory**.)

megablend (also **multiple blend**) While the 'basic' **integration network** consists of four mental spaces: a **generic space**, two **input spaces** and a **blended space**, in reality, it is common, and indeed the norm, for blended spaces to function as inputs for further conceptual blending and reblending. The result of such recursive **conceptual integration** involving numerous input spaces is a megablend. An example of a megablend is the GRIM REAPER blend illustrated in Figure 22.

This is a highly conventional cultural blend in which DEATH is personified as the GRIM REAPER. This blend derives from an integration network consisting of three inputs, one of which is itself a blend consisting of two prior inputs. The Grim Reaper, as depicted in iconography since mediaeval times, is represented as a hooded skeleton holding a scythe.

There are three inputs to the GRIM REAPER blend. These relate to three AGENTS: (1) a REAPER, who uses a scythe to cut down plants; (2) a KILLER, who murders a victim; and (3) DEATH, which brings about the death of an individual. Observe that the third AGENT is

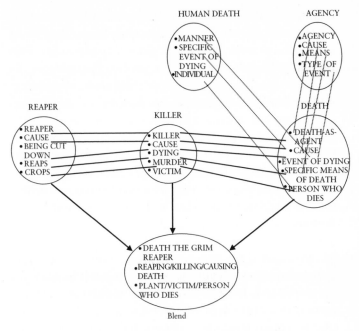

Figure 22. The GRIM REAPER blend

non-human: DEATH is an abstract AGENT. In other words, DEATH-AS-AGENT is itself a **metaphoric blend,** in which DEATH and AGENCY (human animacy and volition) have been blended, giving rise to the personification of death. In the GRIM REAPER blend, the AGENT is DEATH, and this agent causes death by KILLING. The manner of killing is REAPING (the use of the scythe). The reaper is GRIM because death is the outcome of his reaping. The physical appearance of the Grim Reaper metonymically represents each of the three main inputs to the blend. The skeleton stands for DEATH, which is the outcome; the hood that hides the reaper's face represents the concealment that often characterises KILLERS; and the scythe stands for the manner of killing, deriving from the REAPER input. Finally, the Grim Reaper emerges from the blend rather than from any of the input spaces. (See also **Blending Theory**.)

mental space Mental spaces are regions of conceptual space that contain specific kinds of information. They are constructed on the basis of generalised linguistic, pragmatic and cultural strategies for recruiting information. The hallmark of a mental space, as opposed to other cognitive entities such as a conceptual **metaphor**, a **semantic frame**, an **idealised cognitive model** or a **domain (1)**, is that mental spaces are constructed 'on-line', in the moment of speaking or thinking, and can be structured by other cognitive entities including semantic frames, idealised cognitive models or domains by a process known as **schema induction**. Thus a mental space results in a unique and temporary 'packet' of **conceptual structure**, constructed for purposes specific to the ongoing discourse. The principles of mental space formation and the relations or **mappings** established between mental spaces have the potential to yield unlimited meanings. Mental spaces are set up by **space-builders**, and can contain one or more of the following sorts of information type: an **element**, a **property** and a **relation**. Mental space construction begins with the formation of a **base space** relative to which other mental spaces are built. A series of connected mental spaces are referred to as a **mental spaces lattice**. (See also **Access Principle, base space, event space, focus space, Mental Spaces Theory, viewpoint space**.)

mental spaces lattice Once a **mental space** has been constructed, it is linked to the other mental spaces established during discourse. As discourse proceeds, mental

Base

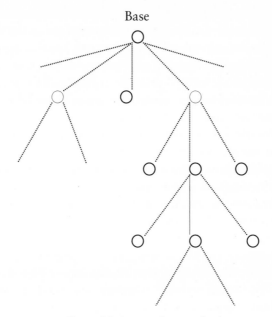

Figure 23. A mental spaces lattice

spaces proliferate giving rise to a mental spaces lattice. This is illustrated in Figure 23.

The circles represent the mental spaces and the dotted lines indicate links between spaces. The **base space** is the first space to be formed in the lattice. (See also **Mental Spaces Theory**.)

Mental Spaces Theory A theory of dynamic meaning-construction developed in particular by *Gilles Fauconnier* and extended in the work of *Seana Coulson, Barbara Dancygier, Eve Sweetser* and others. Mental Spaces Theory also forms the basis for **Blending Theory**. The central insight of Mental Spaces Theory is that when we think and speak, we set up mental spaces. A **mental space** serves to recruit temporary structure from the local discourse context as well as recruiting structure from long-term memory via a process known as **schema induction**. As talk unfolds and thought proceeds, mental spaces proliferate, with new mental spaces being formed relative to others. This gives rise to a **mental spaces lattice**. Language provides conventional prompts for the formation of a given mental space, but mental space construction and the formation of a mental spaces lattice is subject to non-linguistic cognitive principles, especially the **Access Principle** and the **Optimisation Principle**.

Mental Spaces Theory arose as an attempt to account for long-standing problems in philosophy of language. In particular, Mental Spaces Theory sought to account for various problems of linguistic reference. By proposing that discourse is partitioned into distinct mental spaces which contain **counterparts** and **connectors** holding between them, Mental Spaces Theory provided an elegant solution to issues which had previously appeared intractable. (See also **backstage cognition**.)

metaphor (also **conceptual metaphor**) A form of **conceptual projection** involving **mappings** or correspondences holding between distinct conceptual **domains**. Conceptual metaphors often consist of a series of **conventional mappings** which relate aspects of two distinct conceptual domains. The purpose of such a set of mappings is to provide structure from one conceptual domain, the **source domain**, by projecting the structure onto the **target domain**. This allows inferences which hold in the source to be applied to the target. For this reason, conceptual metaphors are claimed to be a basic and indispensable instrument of thought.

For instance, the conceptual metaphor LOVE IS A JOURNEY serves to structure the target domain LOVE in terms of the source domain JOURNEY which allows us to think and talk about love in terms of journeys. A metaphor of this kind is made up of a number of conventional mappings stored in long-term memory. Hence, the travellers from the domain of JOURNEY are conventionally mapped onto that of lovers in the domain of LOVE, the notion of vehicle is mapped onto that of the love relationship and so on, as illustrated below:

source: JOURNEY	$\rightarrow$	target: LOVE
the travellers	$\rightarrow$	the lovers
the vehicle	$\rightarrow$	the love relationship
the journey	$\rightarrow$	events in the relationship
the distance covered	$\rightarrow$	the progress made
the obstacles encountered	$\rightarrow$	the difficulties experienced
decisions about which way to go	$\rightarrow$	choices about what to do
destination of the journey	$\rightarrow$	goals of the relationship

This conceptual metaphor motivates a wide range of linguistic utterances of which the following are illustrative: *Look how far we've come*; *Our relationship is at a crossroads*; *We'll just have to go our separate ways*; *Their marriage has been a long bumpy road*; and so forth. Sentences of this kind, while ostensibly referring to the language of travel, for instance *a bumpy road*, represent a conventional means of describing aspects of a love relationship, for example the difficulties experienced.

Although there are a number of different motivations for, and kinds of, metaphors, **Conceptual Metaphor Theory** emphasises the **experiential basis** of many of the metaphors described. In other words, conceptual metaphors are often grounded in the nature of human interaction with the socio-physical world of **embodied experience**. (See also **compound metaphor, correlation-based metaphor, discourse metaphor, generic-level metaphor, image metaphor, metaphor system, metaphoric entailment, primary metaphor, resemblance-based metaphor, specific-level metaphor**).

metaphor from metonymy One way in which **metaphor** and **metonymy** can interact and thus one kind of the more general phenomenon known as **metaphtonymy**. In this form of interaction, a metaphor is grounded in a metonymic relationship. For example, the expression *close-lipped* can mean 'silent', which follows from metonymy: when one has one's lips closed, one is (usually) silent, therefore to describe someone as *close-lipped* can stand metonymically for silence. However, *close-lipped* can also mean 'speaking but giving little away'. This interpretation is metaphoric, because we understand the absence of meaningful information in terms of silence. The metaphoric interpretation has a metonymic basis, in that it is only because being closed-lipped can stand for silence that the metaphoric reading is possible: thus metaphor from metonymy. (See also **metonymy within metaphor**.)

metaphor system The idea, developed in the work of *George Lakoff* and *Mark Johnson*, that metaphorical language appears to relate to an underlying 'system of thought'. In particular, the conceptual system is held in **Conceptual Metaphor Theory** to be structured by a system of metaphors which work together in order to complement one another and which inherit structure from each other. A good example of this phenomenon is the **Event Structure Metaphor**. (See also **inheritance (1), metaphor**.)

metaphoric blend A **metaphor** analysed from the perspective of **Blending Theory**. From this perspective metaphors involve 'frame-projection asymmetry': while both input spaces contain a distinct frame, it is only the frame from one of these inputs (the **source domain** in **Conceptual Metaphor Theory**, the **framing input** in Blending Theory) that is projected to the **blended space**. Although a **single scope network** is the **prototype** for a metaphoric blend, other kinds of **integration network** can exhibit frame-projection asymmetry to varying degrees and thus can be considered to be metaphoric blends. Such an example is the DIGGING YOUR OWN GRAVE blend, which is discussed in the entry for **double-scope network**.

metaphoric entailment In addition to the **cross-domain mappings** that conceptual metaphors bring with them, they can also provide additional, sometimes quite detailed knowledge. This is because aspects of the **source domain** that are not explicitly stated in the **mappings** can be inferred and mapped onto the source domain by specific linguistic utterances. In this way, metaphoric mappings can carry rich inferences known as metaphoric entailments. Consider the following examples which relate to the conceptual **metaphor** AN ARGUMENT IS A JOURNEY:

1. We will proceed in a *step-by-step fashion*
2. We have *covered a lot of ground*

In this metaphor, PARTICIPANTS in the argument correspond to TRAVELLERS, the ARGUMENT itself corresponds to a JOURNEY and the PROGRESS of the argument corresponds to the ROUTE taken. However, in the source domain JOURNEY, travellers can get lost, they can stray from the path, they can fail to reach their destination and so on. The association between source and target gives rise to the entailment (the obligatory inference) that these events can also occur in the target domain ARGUMENT. This is illustrated by the examples below which illustrate that structure that holds in the source domain can be inferred as holding in the target domain.

3. I *got lost in* the argument
4. We *digressed from* the main point
5. He failed *to reach* the conclusion
6. I *couldn't follow* the argument

(See also **Conceptual Metaphor Theory**.)

metaphorical extension links One of a number of **inheritance links** between constructions posited in **Construction Grammar (2)**. Involves a type of **of inheritance (2)** in which some constructions are metaphorical extensions of other constructions. For instance, in the following utterance: *John gave Mary a kiss*, the independently motivated conceptual **metaphor**: A CAUSAL EVENT IS PHYSICAL TRANSFER motivates the extension of the **ditransitive construction**. That is, ditransitive syntax, which encodes successful physical transfer, is being employed to encode metaphorical transfer of a non-physical entity: *a kiss*. Thus this represents a metaphorical instance of the ditransitive construction and thus is linked to the ditransitive construction by a metaphorical extension link. (See also **construction (1)**.)

metaphtonymy The phenomenon, studied by *Louis Goossens,* in which **metaphor** and **metonymy** interact. While Goossens identified a number of logically possible ways in which metaphor and metonymy could potentially interact, he found that only two of these logically possible interactions were commonly attested. These are known as **metaphor from metonymy** and **metonymy within metaphor**.

metonymic ICM An ICM that comes to stand for the entire category of which it is a member. This can work in two ways. Firstly, an ICM can be a sub-category of a **cluster model** and come to stand for the entire cluster model. For instance, the cluster model for MOTHER may include at least the following ICMs: THE BIRTH MODEL, THE GENETIC MODEL, THE NURTURANCE MODEL, THE MARITAL MODEL and THE GENEALOGICAL MODEL. One of these can, via **metonymy**, come to stand for the entire cluster of ICMs.

Secondly, an individual member of a category can come to stand for the category as a whole giving rise to a metonymic ICM. Metonymic ICMs of this kind include the following: **social stereotypes, typical examples, ideals, paragons, generators** and **salient examples**.

An important consequence of a metonymic ICM is that by standing for the whole category, it serves as a 'cognitive reference point', setting up norms and expectations against which other members of the category are evaluated and assessed. It follows that metonymic ICMs give rise to **typicality effects**, as other members of the category are judged as atypical relative to the metonymic model.

Metonymy (also **conceptual metonymy**) A conceptual operation in which one entity, the **vehicle**, can be employed in order to identify another entity, the **target** (**1**), with which it is associated. As with conceptual **metaphor**, conceptual metonymy licenses linguistic expressions. Consider the following utterance, in which one waitress is addressing another in a restaurant and describes a customer in the following way: *Be careful, the ham sandwich has wandering hands*. This use of the expression *ham sandwich* represents an instance of metonymy: two entities are associated so that one entity (the item the customer ordered) stands for the other (the customer). As this example demonstrates, linguistic metonymy is **referential** in nature: it relates to the use of expressions to 'pinpoint' entities in order to talk about them. This shows that metonymy functions differently from metaphor. For this utterance to be metaphorical we would need to understand *ham sandwich* not as an expression referring to the customer who ordered it but in terms of a food item with human qualities. On this interpretation, we would be attributing human qualities to a ham sandwich, motivated by the metaphor AN INANIMATE ENTITY IS AN AGENT. As these two quite distinct interpretations show, while metonymy is the conceptual relation 'X stands for Y', metaphor is the conceptual relation 'X understood in terms of Y'.

A further key distinction between metonymy and metaphor is that while metaphor involves **cross-domain mapping**s, metonymy involves a mapping within a single **domain (2)** or **domain matrix**. This idea has been developed in particular in the work of *Zoltán Kövecses* and *Günter Radden*. Recent work in cognitive semantics, particularly that associated with *Antonio Barcelona*, has argued that metonymy may be more basic than metaphor and may motivate metaphor. Some conventional conceptual metonymies, with examples, are provided below.

The vehicle is italicised in each case.

PRODUCER FOR PRODUCT
I've just bought a new *Citröen*

Pass me the *Shakespeare* on the top shelf
She likes eating *Burger King*

PLACE FOR EVENT
Iraq nearly cost Tony Blair the premiership
American public opinion fears another *Vietnam*
Let's hope that *Beijing* will be as successful an Olympics
    as *Athens*

PLACE FOR INSTITUTION
Downing Street refused comment
Paris and *Washington* are having a spat
Europe has upped the stakes in the trade war with the
    United States

PART FOR WHOLE
My *wheels* are parked out the back
Lend me *a hand*
She's not just *a pretty face*

WHOLE FOR PART
England beat *Australia* in the 2003 Rugby World Cup
    final
The European Union has just passed new human rights
    legislation
My car has developed a mechanical fault

EFFECT FOR CAUSE
He has *a long face*
He has *a spring in his step* today
Her *face is beaming*

(See also **Domain Highlighting Model, metaphtonymy.**)

metonymy within metaphor One way in which **metaphor**
    and **metonymy** can interact, and thus one kind of the
    more general phenomenon known as **metaphtonymy**.
    To illustrate, consider the following example: *She*

caught the Prime Minister's ear and persuaded him to accept her plan. This example is licensed by the metaphor ATTENTION IS A MOVING PHYSICAL ENTITY, according to which ATTENTION is understood as a MOVING ENTITY that has to be 'caught' (the minister's ear). However, within this metaphor there is also the metonymy EAR FOR ATTENTION, in which EAR is the body part that functions as the vehicle for the concept of ATTENTION in the metaphor. In this example, the instance of metonymy is 'inside' the metaphor. (See also **metaphor from metonymy**.)

micro-sense see **sub-sense**

mimesis (also **bodily mimesis**) According to evolutionary psychologist *Merlin Donald*, a form of cognitive representation that was crucial to the development of the cognitively modern mind, and advanced symbolic abilities such as ritual, narrative, language and so on. Mimesis involves, among other things, the ability to use a body part and the motion associated with the body part in order to represent some action, object or event and, crucially, for this representation to be intended by the subject to stand for the action, object or event in question. Thus mimesis forms the basis for body-based representation and communication. The notion of mimesis has come to be influential in **cognitive linguistics** in terms of the development of the notion of the **mimetic schema**.

mimetic schema A form of body-based representation proposed by *Jordan Zlatev* which builds on the notion of **mimesis** and which is hypothesised to ground linguistic meaning. The mimetic schema is also claimed to be superior to the related construct of **image**

schema. Mimetic schemas have a number of properties associated with them, some of which include: the view that they are based on bodily action and are thus body-based, that they are representational in that they stand for a particular object, action or event, that they are accessible to consciousness, that they are specific, each one constituting a generalisation over a particular bodily act, and finally that they can be pre-reflectively shared, in the sense that they can be imitated and thus 'shared' via cultural exposure.

mirror network   A type of **integration network** in which all the mental spaces in the network share a common **frame,** including the **blended space.** An example of a mirror network is the BOAT RACE blend discussed by *Gilles Fauconnier* and *Mark Turner*. In this blend, the 1993 sea journey by the modern catamaran *Great American II* is conceptualised as a race against the 'ghost' of the clipper *Northern Light* which established a record for the run from San Francisco to Boston in 1853, 140 years earlier. Each **mental space** in this integration network contains the frame in which a boat follows a course. Accordingly, as each mental space reflects the frame contained by the others, for this reason it is given the appellation 'mirror'. For a diagram of the BOAT RACE blend see the entry for **outer-space relation.** (See also **Blending Theory, double scope network, simplex network, single scope network.**)

mode   One of the four **schematic categories** in the **perspectival system.** This category relates to whether a perspective point is in motion or not. This interacts with **distance,** where 'distal' tends to correlate with 'stationary' and 'proximal' with 'moving'. If the perspective point is stationary, it is in 'synoptic mode'. If the perspective point is moving, it is in 'sequential mode'. This is illustrated by the following examples:

1. Max had seen some houses   [synoptic]
    through the car window
2. Max kept seeing houses through   [sequential]
    the car window

The example in (1) invokes the perspective of a fixed vantage point. In contrast, (2) invokes a motion perspective, as a result of which the houses are seen one or some at a time. (See also **conceptual system, direction, location.**)

modular approach An approach informed by the modular theory of mind. This theory, associated in particular with **formal linguistics**, is also explored in other areas of cognitive science such as philosophy and cognitive psychology. It holds that the human mind is organised into distinct 'encapsulated' modules of knowledge, one of which is language, and that these modules serve to 'digest' raw sensory input in such a way that it can then be processed by the central cognitive system (involving deduction, reasoning, memory and so on). Cognitive linguists specifically reject the claim that there is a distinct language module.

The claim that language is an encapsulated module amounts to the assertion that linguistic structure and organisation are markedly distinct from other aspects of cognition. From the perspective of formal linguistics, this theory entails that language can be studied independently of other aspects of cognitive function. Moreover, formal linguists also treat language itself as modular. Thus the various 'knowledge systems' that make up linguistic knowledge, including phonology, semantics and syntax, are encapsulated sub-modules of the language module. Accordingly, they too can be studied independently of one another as they are held to be structured in wholly distinct ways. Cognitive linguists also reject the claim that language consists of wholly distinct sub-modules.

monosemy Associated with work in lexical semantics from the perspective of **formal linguistics**. While formal lexical semanticists have long recognised the existence of **polysemy**, it has generally been viewed as a surface phenomenon, in the sense that lexical entries are underspecified (abstract and lacking in detail), and are 'filled in' either by context as argued by Charles Ruhl, or by the application of certain kinds of lexical generative devices as proposed by James Pustejovsky. According to this view, polysemy is epiphenomenal, emerging from a monosemous lexical entry. According to this monosemy perspective, at the conceptual level a **linguistic unit** such as a word has a single relatively abstract meaning from which other senses (such as the range of meanings associated with **over**) are derived. Work in **cognitive lexical semantics** has typically argued against a monosemy perspective, preferring to view surface polysemy as reflecting conceptual reality.

motivation Relates to **relationships between constructions** in **Construction Grammar (2)**. Specifically, motivation concerns the degree to which the properties of a given **construction (1)** are predictable with respect to another construction. This notion is formalised as the **Principle of Maximised Motivation**. (See also **inheritance (2)**.)

moving ego model An **ego-based cognitive model for time**. In this **cognitive model**, time is a landscape over

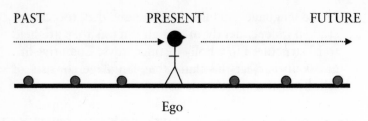

Ego

Figure 24. The moving ego model

which the ego moves, and is understood by virtue of the motion of the ego across this landscape, towards specific temporal moments and events that are conceptualised as locations. As with the **moving time model**, the central inference which arises has to do with the location of temporal events relative to the subjective experience of now. However, in addition, time is conceptualised in terms of units or amounts, by virtue of it being conceptualised in terms of a spatial landscape that can be divided.

This model is illustrated in Figure 24. In the diagram the small circles on the landscape represent future 'times' towards which the ego moves, while 'times' that the ego has already moved beyond now lie in the past. The ego's motion is represented by the direction of the arrow.

Evidence for linguistic encoding of the moving ego model comes from examples such as the following:

1. We're moving towards Christmas
2. We're approaching my favourite part of the piece
3. She's passed the deadline
4. We'll have an answer within two weeks
5. The meetings were spread out over a month

(See also **Aymara, temporal sequence model, time-based cognitive model for time.**)

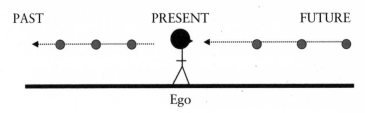

PAST   PRESENT   FUTURE

Ego

Figure 25. The moving time model

moving time model An **ego-based cognitive model for time**. In this **cognitive model,** there is an ego (the subjective experiencer), who may either be implicit or linguistically coded by expressions such as *I*. The ego's location represents the experience of 'now'. In this model, and unlike the **moving ego model,** the ego is static. Temporal moments and events are conceptualised as objects in motion. These objects move towards the ego from the future and then beyond the ego into the past. It is by virtue of this motion that the passage of time is understood. As with the moving ego model, the central inference to derive from this cognitive model has to do with the 'location' of temporal events as being past or future in nature with respect to the ego. This contrasts with the **temporal sequence model** which is concerned not with past/future but rather an earlier/ later relation.

This model is set out diagrammatically in Figure 25. The small dark circles represent 'times', and the arrow connecting the 'times' indicates motion of the 'times' towards and past the ego.

Linguistic evidence for this cognitive model comes from examples such as the following:

1. Christmas is getting closer
2. My favourite part of the piece is coming up

3. The deadline has passed

(See also **Aymara, time-based cognitive model for time.**)

multiple blend see **megablend**

multiplex trajector A **trajector** that involves multiple entities as in the following example: *the sand all over the floor*. The sand here represents a multiple trajector as the example designates all the points in space at which the trajectory, *the sand*, and the **landmark**, *the floor*, are related.

network model In **Cognitive Grammar,** *Ronald Langacker* proposes a network model in order to account for the structure of grammatical categories. In this model, members of a category are viewed as nodes in a complex network, analogous to the notion of the **radial category** associated with *George Lakoff* in the development of **cognitive lexical semantics.** In the network model, the links between nodes in a network arise from a number of different kinds of categorising relationships that hold between the symbolic assemblies stored in the grammatical inventory. One categorising relationship is extension from a **prototype**, represented as [A]⋯▶[B], where A is the prototype and B shares some but not all attributes of A and is thus categorised as an instance of that category. A second type of categorising relationship is **schema-instance organisation**, represented as [A]▶[B]. The **schema** structures those symbolic assemblies related to it as a category within the network, and novel expressions can be compared against such

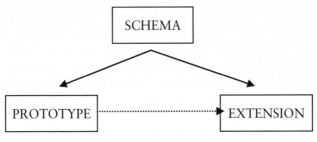

Figure 26. The network model

categories. The network grows 'upwards' via **schematisation** 'outwards' via extension and 'downwards' as more detailed instances are added. Figure 26 illustrates the network model.

Neural Theory of Language A project involving linguists and cognitive scientists attempting to use computational techniques in order to model the way in which the brain gives rise to linguistic organisation and processing. This project adopts the view of language developed in **cognitive linguistics** and is associated with *Jerome Feldman*, *George Lakoff* and their various collaborators.

nominal predication In **Cognitive Grammar,** a nominal predication relates to the **schematic meaning** encoded by nouns and noun phrases (nominals). The term 'predication' relates to meaning and refers to the semantic pole of a **symbolic assembly.** Nominal predications are **conceptually autonomous.** (See also **relational predication.**)

normal replication The linguemes in any given **utterance** are usually associated with a conventional meaning.

Normal replication occurs when linguemes are used in accordance with the **conventions** of the language. (See also **altered replication, lingueme, replicator, Utterance Selection Theory.**)

O

objective construal A form of **construal** in which there is explicit dependence on the **ground** and thus the context of the **utterance**, including participants, time of the speech event and so on. The greater the attention upon the ground, the greater the objectivity of construal. Speaker and hearer are usually subjectively construed or 'off-stage', and only become objectively construed or 'on-stage' when linguistically profiled by expressions such as *I* or *you*. For example, if *Max* utters the first person pronoun *I*, he places himself in the foreground as an object of perception. In this way, the speaker is objectified, giving rise to objective construal. (See also **subjective construal.**)

Objectivist Semantics The general label applied by cognitive linguists (particularly *Gilles Fauconnier, George Lakoff* and *Ronald Langacker* in their writings) to formal approaches to semantics which assume that language refers to a mind-independent 'objective' reality. In contrast, Fauconnier, Lakoff, Langacker and others assume that when language refers to external reality it always does so indirectly, by virtue of referring to concepts which inhere in the **conceptual system**. On this view, the conceptual system constitutes our knowledge-base concerning the world 'out there' and thus our **projected reality**. In essence, cognitive linguists take what is sometimes termed a 'representational' rather than a 'denotational' view of linguistic reference. (See also **cognitive linguistics**.)

open class forms A set of linguistic forms to which it is typically easier for a language to add new members. In English these are nouns, verbs, adjectives and adverbs. In terms of the meaning contributed by the closed class elements they provide **content meaning**. They contribute to the interpretation of an **utterance** by utilising the schematic meaning provided by **closed class forms** in order to provide rich content. (See also **conceptual content system**.)

optimality principles see **governing principles**

Optimisation Principle In **Mental Spaces Theory**, the principle that allows **counterparts** of an **element**, together with properties and relations, to spread through the **mental spaces lattice**. The Optimisation Principle guarantees that structure propagates downwards through the mental spaces lattice, unless the information being propagated is explicitly contradicted by some new information that emerges as the discourse proceeds. This principle enables mental space configurations to build complex structures with a minimum of explicit instructions. (See also **Access Principle, backstage cognition, mental space**.)

overt closed class forms These are **closed class forms** that have conventional phonetic realisation. Overt closed class forms can be bound morphemes (for example, inflectional morphemes such as the -*s* plural marker as in *dogs*) or free morphemes (for example, English determiners such as *the* or *a*, or prepositions such as *in* or **over**). Closed class forms which are overt contrast with **implicit closed class forms**.

outer-space relation In an **integration network**, an outer-space relation is a **vital relation** that holds between **counterparts** across **input spaces**. This contrasts with the notion of an **inner-space relation**.

To illustrate, consider the boat race blend, discussed by *Gilles Fauconnier* and *Mark Turner*, and prompted for by the following utterance: *As we went to press, Rich Wilson and Bill Biewenga were barely maintaining a 4.5 day lead over the ghost of the clipper Northern Light*. This example relates to a 1993 news story in which a modern catamaran *Great American II*, sailed by Wilson and Biewenga, set out on a route from San Francisco to Boston. A record for this route had been set in 1853 by the clipper *Northern Light*, which had made the journey in 76 days and 8 hours. This record still held in 1993. The utterance above prompts for an integration network in which there are two input spaces: one relating to the journey of the modern catamaran in 1993 and the other relating to the original journey undertaken by the *Northern Light* in 1853. The **generic space** contains schematic information relating to BOATS and JOURNEYS, which motivates **matching** and thus cross-space **connectors** between counterparts in the two input spaces. In the **blended space**, we have two boats: *Great American II* and *Northern Light*. Moreover, in the blend the two boats are engaged in a RACE by virtue of **schema induction** which recruits a RACE **frame**. In this boat race blend, the modern catamaran is conceptualised as barely maintaining a lead over the *Northern Light*. The integration network just described is illustrated in Figure 27.

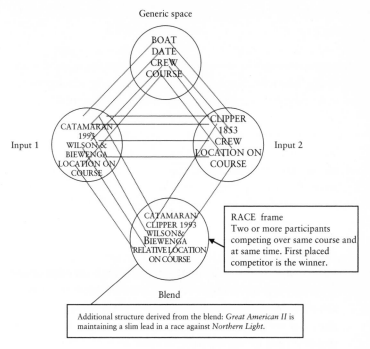

Figure 27. The BOAT RACE blend

The outer-space vital relations are designated by the lines relating counterparts in the input spaces. The vital relation that connects the catamaran/clipper and Wilson and Biewenga/crew is that of IDENTITY. The outer-space vital relation connecting the two dates 1853 and 1993 is that of TIME. The outer-space relation connecting the specific locations on the course of the two boats at any given point during their respective journeys is that of SPACE. (See also **Blending Theory**.)

over One of the most well-studied words of recent times. In a pioneering 1981 Master's thesis *Claudia Brugman*

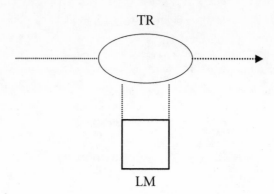

Figure 28. Central image schema for *over*

carried out a detailed study of *over* showing the motivated nature of word-meaning, arguing that *over* could
be analysed as a single category of related or polysemous senses. *George Lakoff* made Brugman's research
famous with his 1987 case study. In particular, Lakoff
argued that *over* could be treated as a **radial category**,
organised with respect to a **prototype,** modelled in
terms of a **semantic network** and exhibiting the phenomenon known as **chaining**. Lakoff argued that the
distinct senses that populated the **semantic network** for
over could be modelled in terms of image schemas, and
that chaining was facilitated by extensions due to conceptual **metaphor** and **image schema transformation**s.
For instance, Lakoff argued that the central image
schema for *over* could be set out diagrammatically as
in Figure 28.

Moreover, he argued that this central image schema
relates to utterances of the following kind: *The plane
flew over*, where TR stands for **trajector**, LM for **landmark** and the arrow signals the direction of the trajector, here the plane.

One consequence of Lakoff's perspective was that he adopted a highly granular approach to **polysemy** known as the **full-specification model**. Work on *over* by Brugman and Lakoff has inspired the research paradigm known as **cognitive lexical semantics**. More recently, other scholars who have worked on *over* include *Andrea Tyler* and *Vyvyan Evans* who in response to problems with Lakoff's account developed the approach known as **Principled Polysemy**.

| P |

paragons   A kind of **metonymic ICM**. Individual category members that represent ideals are **paragons**. For instance, a car manufactured by Rolls-Royce represents a paragon in terms of LUXURY CARS, Nelson Mandela represents a paragon in terms of POLITICAL LEADERS, Winston Churchill in terms of WAR LEADERS, and so on. Because paragons stand for an entire category, they set up norms and expectations against which other members of the category may be evaluated. For instance, the comment, 'He's no Nelson Mandela' about a particular political leader may represent a negative assessment as to the leader's altruism and so forth. In this way, paragons give rise to **typicality effects**. (See also **generators, ideals, salient examples, social stereotypes, typical examples**.)

parameters of focal adjustment   There are three parameters along which a **focal adjustment** can vary. The three parameters are: (1) **selection**; (2) **perspective**; and (3) **abstraction (2)**. Together, these parameters provide different ways of focusing attention upon, and thus providing a unique **construal** of, a scene. This is set out diagrammatically in Figure 29.

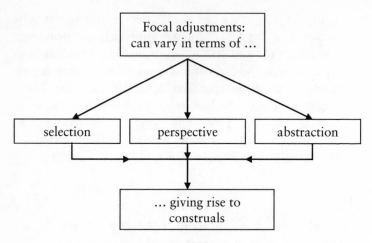

Figure 29. The relationship between focal adjustments and construal

participant roles In **Construction Grammar (2)**, the 'slots' encoded by a particular verb which determine what participant types can be combined with the verb. This follows from the assumption that the semantics of any verb are relativised to a **semantic frame**. The semantic frame is, in turn, held to determine the participants that can be associated with the verb. For example, the verb *buy* might be associated with the participant roles BUYER, SELLER and GOODS, while the verb *sing* might be associated with the participant roles SINGER and SONG. (See also **argument roles, fusion (1)**.)

pattern One of the factors which governs the **attentional system** in the **conceptual structuring system**. Relates to the way in which patterns of attention are organised. There are three kinds of pattern: **focus of attention, window of attention** and **level of attention**. (See also **Conceptual Structuring System Approach, mapping, strength**.)

Table 10. Pattern of distribution

Pattern of distribution	*Example*
One-way non-resettable	*(to) die*
One-way resettable	*(to) fall*
Full-cycle	*(to) flash*
Multiplex	*(to) breathe*
Steady-state	*(to) sleep*

pattern completion see **completion**

pattern of distribution One of the **schematic categories** in
the **configurational system**. Pattern of distribution
relates to how matter is distributed through SPACE, or
how action is distributed through TIME. This category
is illustrated in Table 10 by action through time as
encoded by verbs.

These patterns can be explained as follows. While
dying represents a change of state from which its participant cannot emerge, falling represents a change of
state from which its participant can emerge (if you fall
you can get up again). If a light flashes, it goes from
dark to light and back to dark again, which represents
a cyclical change of state. Repeating the cycle is not an
intrinsic part of flashing (because a light can flash only
once), while it is an intrinsic part of breathing. In contrast to all of these, which involve some internal
change, sleep represents a steady or unchanging state.
(See also **axiality, boundedness, Conceptual Structuring
System Approach, degree of extension, dividedness,
plexity, schematic systems.**)

pattern-finding ability One of two general cognitive skills
that enables humans to acquire language. This ability allows humans to recognise patterns and perform

'statistical' analysis over sequences of perceptual input, including the auditory stream that constitutes spoken language. Pre-linguistic infants – children under a year old – employ this ability in order to abstract across utterances and find repeated patterns that allow them to construct linguistic units. It is this pattern-finding ability that underlies the **abstraction** process assumed in **Cognitive Grammar**.

Infant pattern-finding skills are not limited to language. Researchers have also found that infants demonstrate the same skills when the experiment is repeated with non-linguistic tone sequences and with visual, as opposed to auditory, sequences. Moreover, this pattern-finding ability appears not to be limited to humans but is also apparent in other primates. For instance, Tamarin monkeys demonstrate the same pattern-recognition abilities when exposed to the same kinds of auditory and visual sequencing experiments described above for human infants. According to *Michael Tomasello*, the ability to acquire high-level symbolic behaviour such as language is a function, therefore, of a further ability that humans but other primates do not possess. This constitutes an **intention-reading ability**. (See also **emergentism**, **linguistic unit**, **socio-cognitive mechanisms in language acquisition**, **utterance**).

perception Involves human sensory (or sense-perceptory) systems and the brain in order to form representations known as percepts. Perception consists of three stages: (1) sensation; (2) perceptual organisation; and (3) identification and recognition.

Sensation concerns the way in which external energy, such as light, heat or (sound) vibrations, are converted into the neural codes which the brain recognises.

Perceptual organisation concerns the way in which this sensory information is organised and formed into a perceptual object, a percept. Identification and recognition relates to the stage in the process whereby past experiences and conceptual knowledge is brought to bear in order to interpret the percept. For instance, a spherical object might be identified and recognised as a football or a coin or a wheel or some other object. That is, this stage involves meaning, which is to say understanding the nature, function and significance of the percept. As such, a previously formed **concept** is employed in order to identify and categorise the percept. (See also **sensory experience**.)

perceptual meaning analysis The mechanism whereby perceptual stimuli are redescribed from perceptual arrays into rudimentary representations which support more complex concepts. The term was coined by developmental psychologist *Jean Mandler*, who argues that perceptual meaning analysis represents the means whereby in early infancy children develop the fundamental plank of the **conceptual system** known as the **image schema**. Perceptual meaning analysis takes place when perceptual arrays of particular kinds are observed to co-occur with particular functional consequences. For instance, a functional consequence of spatial arrays involving three-dimensional volumetric entities is that they provide a support/containment function. This information, which is distinct in kind from the purely sensory information with which it is associated, comes to form the rudimentary concept CONTAINER.

perspectival system One of the four **schematic systems** which form part of the **conceptual structuring system**.

The perspectival system establishes a viewpoint from which participants and scenes are viewed and involves four **schematic categories**. These are **location, distance, mode** and **direction**. These can be encoded by **closed class forms**. (See also **attentional system, Conceptual Structuring System Approach, configurational system, force-dynamics system, schematic categories**.)

perspective One of the three **parameters of focal adjustment**. Relates to the way in which a scene is viewed, including the relative prominence of its participants. The case of an active and passive pair of sentences illustrates this point:

1. Max ate all the tomato soup   [active]
2. All the tomato soup was eaten by Max   [passive]

In example (1) the focal participant, the **trajector**, is *Max* who is the AGENT of the action, and the secondary participant, the **landmark**, is *the soup* which is the PATIENT. In (2) the situation is reversed, and the PATIENT is now the focal participant, the trajector. In a passive sentence, the AGENT is the secondary participant, the landmark. The distinction between these two sentences relates to a shift in perspective which is effected by changing the relative prominence attached to the participants in the **profiled relationship**. (See also **abstraction (2), construal, focal adjustment, selection**.)

plexity One of the **schematic categories** in the **configurational system**. Plexity relates to whether a quantity of TIME or SPACE consists of one (uniplex) or more than one (multiplex) equivalent elements. When related to SPACE (or matter), this is the basis of the grammatical category number. For instance, the singular count noun *slipper* represents uniplex structure, while the plural count noun *slippers* represents multiplex structure. Mass nouns like *champagne* also have multiplex structure. When related to the domain of TIME (or action), plexity forms part of the basis for the distinction in lexical aspect between semelfactive (one instance) versus iterative (repeated instances). This is illustrated below:

1. Max coughed   [semelfactive]
2. Max coughed for ten minutes   [iterative]

The verb *cough* encodes a **punctual** event, and thus encodes semelfactive aspect which has uniplex structure. When a punctual event is drawn out over a period of time, as in the second example, it becomes iterative. Iterative lexical aspect has multiplex structure. (See also **axiality, boundedness, Conceptual Structuring System Approach, degree of extension, dividedness, pattern of distribution, schematic systems.**)

polysemy The phenomenon whereby a **linguistic unit** exhibits multiple distinct yet related meanings. Traditionally, this term is restricted to the study of word-meaning (lexical semantics), where it is used to describe words like *body* which has a range of distinct, meanings that are nevertheless related (for example, the human body, a corpse, the trunk of the human body, the main or central part of something).

Cognitive linguists claim that polysemy is not restricted to word-meaning but is a fundamental feature of human language. According to this view, the 'distinct' areas of language all exhibit polysemy. Cognitive linguists therefore view polysemy as a key to generalisation across a range of 'distinct' phenomena and argue that polysemy reveals important fundamental commonalities between lexical, morphological and syntactic organisation.

Polysemy has been explored in greatest detail in the branch of **cognitive linguistics** known as **cognitive lexical semantics**. Scholars working in this area assume that polysemy is a conceptual rather than a purely linguistic phenomenon. That is, linguistic polysemy patterns reflect, and therefore reveal, systematic differences and patterns in the way linguistic units are organised and structured in the mind. For this reason, the study of polysemy has been of particular interest to cognitive lexical semanticists and has resulted in a vast literature of detailed studies on linguistic units of various sorts including the most famous set of studies of all on the English preposition **over**. (See also **homonymy, monosemy**.)

polysemy fallacy A fallacy in reasoning committed by some scholars who take a **cognitive lexical semantics** approach, particularly as evident in the **full-specification model** of polysemy. *Dominiek Sandra*, who coined the phrase, argues that to view all context-bound usages of a particular lexical item as instances of polysemy is to commit what he calls the polysemy fallacy. The fallacy can be paraphrased as follows: because a lexical item exhibits distinct semantic contributions in context, each distinct semantic contribution is due to a distinct underlying sense or **lexical concept**. According to Sandra this reasoning is fallacious as it does not follow that all or even many distinct instances associated with a lexical item provide evidence for distinct senses stored in semantic memory. The polysemy fallacy then serves to underplay the role of context in providing a **linguistic unit** with a semantic value.

polysemy links One of a number of **inheritance links** between constructions posited in **Construction**

Grammar (2). Involves a type of **inheritance (2)** in which a construction with a similar syntactic organisation to another exhibits a distinct but related meaning. For example, the **ditransitive construction** is associated with a range of senses that all share the semantics of TRANSFER, but which also differ in systematic ways. The examples below illustrate some of the distinct polysemous senses associated with this construction:

1. X CAUSES Y TO RECEIVE Z
   Max gave Bella a biscuit
2. CONDITIONS OF SATISFACTION IMPLY X CAUSES Y TO RECEIVE Z
   Max promised Bella a biscuit
3. X ENABLES Y TO RECEIVE Z
   Max allowed Bella a biscuit
4. X CAUSES Y NOT TO RECEIVE Z
   Max refused Bella a biscuit
5. X INTENDS TO CAUSE Y TO RECEIVE Z
   Max made Bella some biscuits
6. X ACTS TO CAUSE Y TO RECEIVE Z AT SOME FUTURE POINT IN TIME
   Max commissioned Bella some fairy-shaped biscuits

(See also **construction (1), constructional polysemy.**)

pragmatic strengthening A notion developed by *Elizabeth Closs Traugott* in work on semantic change and applied and developed in the theory of **Principled Polysemy** in attempting to account for how **chaining** takes place in a **semantic network**. Takes a usage-based perspective on chaining: context-dependent inferences associated with a given word are reanalysed as distinct meanings. Through a process of strengthening, these 'new' meanings come to be stored as distinct senses or lexical concepts in semantic memory. This process is thus referred to as pragmatic strengthening. For instance, *Vyvyan Evans* and *Andrea Tyler* in their work on English prepositions argue that pragmatic strengthening gives rise to the development of new prepositional meanings. In an utterance such as: *The tablecloth is over the table*, a context-dependent inference is that a consequence of the tablecloth being 'over' (i.e. 'above'), the table it also covers the table. The inference of 'covering' has, via reanalysis and strengthening, come to be stored in long-term memory as a distinct 'covering' meaning conventionally indexed by the form **over**. Evans and Tyler argue that it is for this reason that *over* can be used to mean 'covering' even where over does not have an 'above' reading, as in examples such as: *The clouds are over the sun.*

primary metaphor The foundational level of metaphoric representation and the central construct in **Primary Metaphor Theory**. A primary metaphor, in contrast to a conceptual **metaphor**, relates distinct concepts rather than sets of concepts. However, like conceptual metaphor, a primary metaphor relates two distinct concepts that occur in distinct domains. Thus a primary metaphor involves a single **cross-domain mapping**.

Primary metaphors are motivated by three necessary and jointly sufficient conditions. Firstly, the association between a target concept and a source concept in a primary metaphor is directly motivated by a tight and recurring correlation in experience. That is, the target and source in a primary metaphor co-vary in experience. Thus a primary metaphor can be characterised as a **correlation-based metaphor**.

Secondly, primary metaphors are formed by an unconscious and thus pre-conceptual association between two elements (primary target and source concepts) which have different kinds of content. While a given **primary target concept** relates to an aspect of **sensory experience** and has what is referred to as 'image content', a **primary source concept** constitutes a subjective response or evaluation of the aspect of sensory experience with respect to which it co-varies. Thus primary source concepts have what is referred to as 'response content'. Put another way, the second condition for a primary metaphor concerns the conventional pairing of response and image content.

The third condition constitutes the requirement that the primary source and target concepts share **super-schematic structure**. This is known as the **Superschema Rule**.

Primary metaphors can give rise to a more complex **compound metaphor** through a process known as **unification**. Due to the highly schematic nature of primary metaphors they are akin to the notion of **generic-level metaphor** in **Conceptual Metaphor Theory**. Examples of primary metaphors are given below:

1. SIMILARITY IS NEARNESS
   That colour is quite close to the one on our dining room wall
2. IMPORTANCE IS SIZE
   We've got a big week coming up at work
3. QUANTITY IS VERTICAL ELEVATION
   The price of shares has gone up
4. CAUSES ARE FORCES
   Vanity drove me to have the operation
5. CHANGE IS MOTION
   Things have shifted a little since you were last here

6. DESIRE IS HUNGER
   We're hungry for a victory

Primary Metaphor Theory A recent approach to conceptual **metaphor** associated with *Joseph Grady* which attempts to resolve some outstanding problems with the account provided by **Conceptual Metaphor Theory**. The fundamental claim is that there are two distinct kinds of metaphor: **primary metaphor** and **compound metaphor**. While primary metaphors are foundational, compound metaphors are constructed from the **unification** of primary metaphors through the process of **conceptual integration**. Grady's central claim, which marks his approach as distinct from earlier work in Conceptual Metaphor Theory, is that primary metaphors conventionally associate concepts that are equally 'basic', in the sense that they are both directly experienced and perceived. This means that Grady rejects the view that the distinction between the target and source of a metaphoric **cross-domain mapping** relates to abstract versus concrete concepts. Instead, Primary Metaphor Theory holds that the distinction between target and source relates to 'degree of subjectivity' rather than how clearly delineated or how abstract a concept is. This view means that the **Invariance Principle** is redundant, because the foundational primary metaphors, upon which more complex metaphor systems are based, are not viewed as providing an 'abstract' target with 'missing' structure.

primary reference object see **reference object**.

primary source concept In a **primary metaphor**, the concept which serves to structure a **primary target concept**. Primary source concepts are relatively simple

aspects of **sensory experience,** such as MOTION, VERTI-
CAL ELEVATION, PROXIMITY, HUNGER, WARMTH, etc.
They are held to constitute redescriptions of specific
aspects of **sensory experience** and are correlated with
subjective evaluations and responses (primary target
concepts). Accordingly they are held to be comprised
of what is referred to as 'image content', which relates
to the idea that primary source concepts derive from
sense-perception of the external world. (See also
Primary Metaphor Theory.)

primary target concept In a **primary metaphor,** the concept which is structured by virtue of a cognitive link
with a **primary source concept.** Primary target concepts are relatively simple, phenomenologically real
aspects of subjective experience, such as TIME, QUAN-
TITY, SIMILARITY, DESIRE, INTIMACY, etc. They are held
to constitute subjective evaluations or responses to
sensory experience with respect to which they are correlated. Accordingly they are held to be comprised of
what is referred to as 'response content' (or sometimes
'subjective content'). (See also **Primary Metaphor
Theory.**)

primitives Innately prescribed, non-reducible units of linguistic organisation assumed by the various theories that
are subsumed under **formal linguistics,** including formal
approaches to grammar, meaning and phonology.

Principle of Linguistic Relativity see **linguistic relativity.**

Principle of Maximised Motivation The principle in **Construction Grammar (2)** which accounts for the **motivation** exhibited by constructions. This principle states
that if one construction is syntactically similar to

another then it is motivated to the degree that it is semantically similar to the other construction. (See also **construction (1)**, **relations between constructions**.)

Principled Polysemy A model of lexical representation developed within **cognitive lexical semantics**. Principled Polysemy was developed by *Vyvyan Evans* and *Andrea Tyler* in response to perceived shortcomings with the **full-specification model** of **polysemy**. In particular, a central concern of Principled Polysemy is to provide a methodologically motivated and principled way of conducting lexical semantic analysis, thereby avoiding the **polysemy fallacy**. Principled Polysemy seeks to develop clear decision principles that make **semantic network** analyses objective and verifiable. These decision principles aim to achieve two goals: (1) they should serve to determine what counts as a distinct sense and thus distinguish between senses stored in semantic memory and context-dependent meanings constructed 'on-line'; (2) they should establish the prototypical or central sense associated with a particular **radial category**. The Principled Polysemy model has been successfully applied to a range of lexical classes including prepositions, nouns and verbs, and several languages in addition to English including Russian and Greek. (See also **contrast set**, **pragmatic strengthening**, **proto-scene**.)

process see **temporal relations**

processing time A term coined by *Ronald Langacker* to refer to the cognitive representation of TIME, where time is a medium of **conceptualisation**. In this sense processing time is 'real time', in the sense that any cognitive process requires processing time. Processing time contrasts with **conceived time**.

profile The entity or relation designated by a word. The profile functions by highlighting a substructure within a larger unit known as the **base**. Take the example *hypotenuse*. This word profiles the longest side in a right-angled triangle, while the base is the entire triangle, including all three of its sides. Without the base, the profile would be meaningless: there is no hypotenuse without a right-angled triangle. Hence the word *hypotenuse* designates a particular substructure within a larger conceptual structure. (See also **profile determinant, profiled relationship, profiling, scope of predication.**)

profile determinant In **Cognitive Grammar**, the head of a **construction (2)**. The 'head' of a phrase is a single word that determines the categorical status of the phrase (for example, a noun heads a noun phrase). Consider the following example: *a girl at the bus stop knitting a scarf*. This phrase contains a number of word-level constituents including three nouns: *girl*, the compound noun *bus stop* and *scarf*. However, only one of these heads the phrase, namely *girl*. Thus this noun serves to determine the profile of the entire phrase, meaning that the entire phrase is a noun phrase. Thus this noun is the profile determinant.

profiled relationship In **Cognitive Grammar**, a linguistically encoded relationship between two or more participants in a given scene. For instance, in an utterance such as: *Max kicked the ball*, there is a profiled relationship holding between the participants encoded by the expressions *Max* and *the ball*. In a profiled relationship there is a conceptual asymmetry between a focal participant, the **trajector** and a secondary participant, the **landmark**. This distinction between trajector

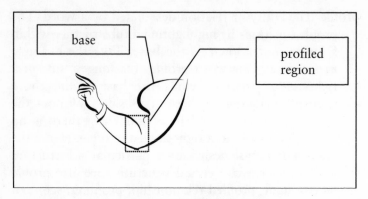

Figure 30. Profiling of *elbow*

and landmark in linguistic expressions is an instance of the more general perceptual and attentional phenomenon of **figure-ground organisation**. In the utterance above, *Max* constitutes the trajector while *the ball* constitutes the landmark. (See also **trajector-landmark organisation**.)

profiling In **Cognitive Grammar**, the conceptual 'highlighting' of some aspect of a **domain (1)**. Specifically, profiling is the process whereby an aspect of some **base** is selected. For example, the expression *elbow* profiles a substructure within the larger structure ARM, which is its base. This idea is illustrated by Figure 30.

projected reality A term coined by *Ray Jackendoff*. Relates to the human construal of reality which is determined by the specifics of human cognitive, neurological and perceptual mechanisms and processes. From this perspective, what we experience as reality is not an objective 'god's eye' view of the world, but the world as constructed by virtue of our species-specific cognitive apparatus and bodies. In this sense reality 'for us' is projected. This notion is compatible with the cognitive linguistic view of **embodied cognition** and stands in opposition to **objectivist semantics**. (See also **experiential realism, variable embodiment**.)

projector-based reference frame As with the **guide-post reference frame**, this **reference frame** also involves an **external secondary reference object**. In this type of reference frame, the **secondary reference object** is an animate entity, whose location serves as a frame of reference in locating the relevant part of the **primary reference object** enabling the **figure** to be located. For instance, in the following example: *The grocery store is to the right of the office building*, the speaker 'projects' his or her bodily horizontal asymmetry (left/right axis) onto the primary reference object (*the office building*) in order to locate the figure (*the grocery store*). It is because the speaker projects **axial properties** onto the reference object in this way that this reference frame is referred to as projector-based. (See also **figure-ground segregation, region, spatial relation, spatial scene**.)

propagation The selection and use of a particular utterance containing a particular **lingueme** or set of linguemes which diffuses a particular **altered replication** (the innovation) through a linguistic community. In time, this innovation becomes established as a new linguistic convention or set of **conventions**. (See also **normal replication, replicator, Utterance Selection Theory**.)

property In **Mental Spaces Theory**, a **property** can be assigned to an **element** in a given **mental space**. In the following sentence: *In that play, Othello is jealous*, the

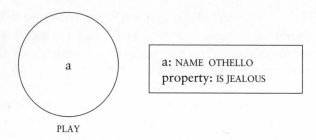

PLAY

Figure 31. Mental space representation for: *Othello is jealous*

expression *In that play* is a space-builder and sets up a mental space. The expression *Othello* assigns an element to the mental space, while **is jealous** assigns the property of jealousy to the element.

In Figure 31 the mental space is set out using a circle. This mental space is labelled PLAY to show that the mental space represents the 'world' inside the play. The name *Othello* introduces an element into the mental space, which we label a, and the expression *jealous* assigns a property to the element (JEALOUS). This information is captured in the 'dialogue box' next to the mental space. (See also **relation, role-value readings.**)

proto-scene In the **Principled Polysemy** model of lexical representation the central sense for a preposition such as **over** is directly grounded in a specific kind of recurring **spatial scene**. This spatial scene, which relates a spatial **trajector** and a **landmark** in a particular spatio-geometric configuration, is called the proto-scene. While the proto-scene is a type of **image schema**, it is distinct from the central image schema proposed for *over* in *George Lakoff*'s **full-specification model** because it relates to a distinct and discrete spatial scene. The proto-scene for *over* is illustrated in Figure 32. The small circle represents the trajector (TR) and

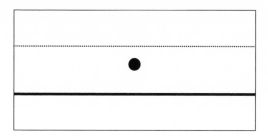

Figure 32. Proto-scene for *over*

the unbroken line the landmark (LM). The fact that the TR is located above the LM indicates that the spatio-geometric relation involves a 'higher than' or ABOVE relation. The dashed line indicates that the TR must be within a region proximal to the LM.

prototype A relatively abstract mental representation that assembles the key attributes or features that best represent instances of a given category. Accordingly, the prototype is viewed as a schematic representation of the most salient or central characteristics associated with members of the category in question. According to **Prototype Theory**, the prototype provides structure to and serves to organise a given category, a phenomenon known as **prototype structure**. An important consequence of this is that categories exhibit **typicality effects**.

prototype structure Relates to the occurrence of repeated attributes across distinct members, or exemplars, of a particular category which gives rise to a **prototype**. Prototype structure thus concerns the degree to which redundancy in the category members is employed in categorisation, by virtue of providing a salient set of attributes that organise the category. Prototype structure also gives rise to **typicality effects**. Prototype structure can be investigated using **goodness-of-example ratings**. (See also **Prototype Theory**.)

Prototype Theory A theory of human categorisation that was posited by *Eleanor Rosch* in order to account for experimental findings that she and her colleagues uncovered during the 1970s. Prototype Theory holds that there are two basic principles that guide the formation of categories in the human mind: (1) the principle of cognitive economy; and (2) the principle of perceived world structure. These principles together give rise to the human categorisation system.

The first principle, the principle of cognitive economy, states that an organism like a human being attempts to gain as much information as possible about its environment while minimising cognitive effort and resources. This cost-benefit balance drives category formation. In other words, rather than storing separate information about every individual stimulus experienced, humans can group similar stimuli into categories, which maintains economy in cognitive representation. The consequence of this is that humans privilege categories formed at a certain level of informational inclusiveness or complexity. This level of categorisation is known as the **basic level** of categorisation.

The second principle, the principle of perceived world structure, posits that the world around us has **correlational structure**. For instance, it is a fact about the world that wings most frequently co-occur with feathers and the ability to fly (as in birds) rather than with fur or the ability to breathe underwater. This principle states that humans rely upon correlational structure of this kind in order to form and organise categories. This correlational structure gives rise to a **prototype**. Since the 1970s Rosch's findings and claims have been called into question. Today, Prototype Theory is no longer seen as an accurate view of categorisation. Nevertheless, it was historically important for the development of **cognitive semantics** (See also **prototype structure, typicality effects.**)

protracted duration The phenomenologically real experience in which time 'feels' as if it is proceeding 'more slowly' than usual. This experience is attested in situations when more of the perceptual stimulus array is attended to, including situations such as novelty, shock, boredom and near-death experiences. It is evident linguistically in expressions such as: *Time seemed to stand still, The time dragged by*, and so forth. In **cognitive linguistics** protracted duration has been studied in detail by *Vyvyan Evans*. (See also **temporal compression.**)

purport A term coined by *Alan Cruse*. Relates to the **encyclopaedic knowledge** associated with a given word. Includes the past uses to which a word has been put. In this regard purport is similar to the notion of **meaning potential**. (See also **semantic potential.**)

R

radial category A category whose members are organised with respect to a **composite prototype**. The members of the radial category are not generated. Rather, they are extended by convention and therefore must be learned. The composite prototype determines the possibilities for the extensions, together with the possible relations between variants and the central prototype.

An important line of research in **cognitive lexical semantics** has been to treat words as radial categories organised with respect to a composite prototype. The most famous work in this vein has been carried out on the English preposition **over**. Radial categories are modelled in terms of a **semantic network**.

Radical Construction Grammar (also **RCG**) A theory of construction grammar developed by *William Croft*. Radical Construction Grammar (RCG) sets out to explore the implications of linguistic typology for syntactic theory. Linguistic typology is the subdiscipline of linguistics that examines the structural properties of language from a cross-linguistic perspective and describes patterns of similarity as well as observing points of diversity. In RCG, rather than taking grammatical universals across the world's languages as a starting point and building a model of language that assumes a universal grammar (as in **formal linguistics**), grammatical diversity is taken as the starting point. RCG attempts to build a model of grammar which accounts adequately for patterns of typological variation.

What makes Croft's constructional approach 'radical' emerges as a consequence of the typological stance he adopts. In RCG, the existence of constructions is the only primitive theoretical construct. All other linguistic elements, including word classes such as nouns and verbs, word order patterns and grammatical relations such as subject and object are epiphenomenal. In this way, the notion of syntax, as usually understood, is eradicated from the theory altogether. (See also **construction grammars**.)

RCG see **Radical Construction Grammar**

reference frame Represents the means language has at its disposal for using a **reference object** in order to locate a **figure**. A reference frame serves to locate the figure by virtue of establishing a **spatial relation** holding between the figure and a reference object. This is achieved by utilising **axial properties** associated with the reference object in order to establish the direction and relative proximity of the figure with respect to the reference object. There is a limited set of reference frames employed by the world's languages. These can be divided into (1) reference frames that involve the reference object alone: a **ground-based reference frame;** and (2) reference frames that also involve a **secondary reference object.** There are three reference frames of this kind: **field-based reference frame, guidepost-based reference frame** and **projector-based reference frame.**

reference object (also **ground**) The less salient element in **figure-ground organisation.** Developed in cognitive linguistics in particular by *Leonard Talmy* in his **Conceptual Structuring System Approach.** (See also **figure, Gestalt psychology, landmark.**)

reference point A notion developed in recent work in **Cognitive Grammar.** Relates to the ability to utilise the idea of one entity in order to invoke or 'get at' another which is closely related. To illustrate, consider the following example: *You know that girl who works part-time in the Dean's office? Well, her room-mate is having an affair with a much older married man from out of town.* In this example the 'girl who works in the Dean's office' is being employed as a reference point in order to get at or 'make contact' with another entity, in this case her roommate. Key to developing the

Cognitive Grammar account of reference point phenomena are the theoretical notions of **target** (2) and **dominion**.

region That part of a **spatial scene** in which the **figure** may be found. A region is established by virtue of a **spatial relation** being designated as holding between a figure and **reference object**. (See also **reference frame, search domain.**)

reification An example of a **conceptual conversion operation**. Relates to the operation that converts our **conceptualisation** of TIME (or action) into SPACE (or matter): an act can be converted into an object or an activity into a mass. When a temporal **concept** is reified, it is expressed by a nominal expression (a noun phrase). Compare the examples in (1) and (2).

	An act	*reified as an object*	*(discrete)*
1.	John washed her	John gave her a wash	
	Activity	*reified as a mass*	*(continuous)*
2.	John helped her	John gave her some help	

In example (1), *washed* is a verb and encodes an act, while *a wash* is a noun phrase and encodes an act conceptualised as an object. In example (2), *helped* is a verb and encodes an activity, while *some help* is a noun phrase and encodes an activity conceptualised as a mass. When an act is construed as an object, it can be described in terms consistent with the properties of objects. For example, *to call (on the phone)* becomes *he gave me a call*; *to slap* becomes *he gave her two slaps*.

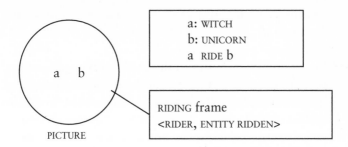

Figure 33. Mental space representation of a relation

relation In **Mental Spaces Theory,** a relation can be assigned as holding between elements in a given **mental space.** In the following sentence: *In the picture, a witch is riding a unicorn,* the expression *In the picture* is a space-builder and sets up a **mental space.** The expressions *a witch* and *a unicorn* assign two elements to the mental space, while *is riding* prompts for a RIDING **frame** (or schema) to structure the mental space. This is achieved via **schema induction.** Once present, the roles associated with the RIDING frame are mapped onto the two elements, establishing a relation between them. While the witch element is associated with the RIDER role, the UNICORN element is associated with the RIDEE role.

In Figure 33 the mental space is set out diagrammatically using a circle. This mental space is labelled PICTURE to show that the mental space represents the 'world' inside the picture. The expression *a witch* introduces an element into the mental space, which we label a, and the expression *a unicorn* introduces a second element which we label b. The relation holding between the two elements is captured by the expression a RIDE b. The riding frame, recruited by schema induction, is represented in the lower dialogue box. (See also **property, role-value readings**.)

relational predication In **Cognitive Grammar**, a relational predication relates to the **schematic meaning** encoded by lexical classes such as verbs, adjectives, prepositions and so on (relations). The term 'predication' relates to meaning and refers to the semantic pole of a **symbolic assembly**. Relational predications are **conceptually dependent**. Relational predications are divided into two sub-categories: **temporal relations** and **atemporal relations**. (See also **nominal predication**.)

relationships between constructions In **Construction Grammar (2)**, the **constructicon** consists of a network of constructions and relationships between them. Relationships between constructions are captured in terms of **inheritance (2)** and **motivation**.

relationships between symbolic assemblies In **Cognitive Grammar**, the set of interlinking and overlapping relationships holding between symbolic assemblies. There are three kinds of relationships that constitute the network: (1) symbolisation – the symbolic links between the semantic pole and phonological pole of a given **symbolic assembly**; (2) categorisation – for example, the link between the expressions *rose* and *flower*, given that ROSE is a member of the category FLOWER; and (3) integration – the relation between parts of a **complex** symbolic assembly such as *flower-s*.

replicator An element of language realised in an **utterance**. A central construct in **Utterance Selection Theory**. (See also **altered replication, lingueme, normal replication**.)

resemblance-based metaphor A **metaphor** based on a perceived resemblance between two entities rather than being motivated by **embodied experience**. Resemblance-based metaphor thus contrasts with **correlation-based metaphor**. An example of a resemblance-based metaphor is the following: *Achilles is a lion*. In this case, the perceived resemblance between Achilles, the Greek warrior, and a lion is not physical: Achilles does not actually look like a lion. Instead, due to cultural knowledge which holds that lions are courageous, by describing Achilles as a lion we associate him with the lion's qualities of courage and ferocity. Thus the perceived resemblance relates to behavioural qualities associated with both Achilles and lions. (See also **image metaphor**.)

resultative construction One of the **verb argument constructions** studied by *Adele Goldberg* in the development of her theory of **Construction Grammar (2)**. The resultative construction is illustrated by the examples below:

1. They shouted themselves hoarse
2. He drank himself unconscious

The construction has the following semantics: X CAUSES Y TO BECOME Z, where X corresponds to the AGENT (subject) NP, Y to the PATIENT (object) NP and Z to the RESULT argument, which may be realised either by an adjective phrase (AP) like *hoarse* (1) or by a preposition phrase (PP). The properties associated with the resultative construction are summarised in Table 11. (See also **construction (1)**.)

role reversal imitation The third aspect of the human **intention-reading ability**, central to first language acquisition. Infants who understand that people manifest

Table 11. Properties of the English resultative construction

The English resultative construction
Subject argument has to be an animate AGENT
Object argument has to be a PATIENT (which thus can undergo a change of state)
Verb has to encode direct causation
Resultative adjective has to designate the endpoint of a scale
Resultative adjective cannot be deverbal

intentional behaviour may attend to and learn (by imitation) the behavioural means that others employ to signal their intentional state. For example, the child may imitate the use of the word *rubber duck* by an adult in directing attention to an object. However, this process does not just involve imitation, but the recognition that by uttering this phrase, the infant can perform a role reversal, thereby signalling a communicative intention: that the adult attend to the toy. (See also **communicative intention, joint attention frame, pattern-finding ability, socio-cognitive mechanisms in first language acquisition.**)

role-value readings The observation in **Mental Spaces Theory** that ambiguities which arise in noun phrases (NPs) with definite reference are due to the NP possessing two possible readings: one relating to a role and one to a value. Consider the following example: *Your car is always different.* This could mean that every time I see your car, some aspect of the car has changed; it might have had a respray, acquired some new hubcaps and so on. Alternatively, this sentence could mean that you have a new car every time I see you. The first reading is the value reading: some aspect or 'value' associated with the same entity has changed. The second reading is the role reading: the entity itself is different.

running the blend see **elaboration (1)**.

rule/list fallacy A term coined by *Ronald Langacker* to describe a specific instance of the **exclusionary fallacy**. To commit the rule/list fallacy is to exclude, for instance, listing a unit such as a word if there is a rule which can predict the lexical unit. This line of reasoning is fallacious as it adopts the view that one must posit either rules or lists but not both. Langacker argues that there is a third choice: to posit rules and lists.

| S |

salient examples A kind of **metonymic ICM**. Memorable or salient examples belonging to a particular category give rise to this type of ICM. For instance, Oxford University is a salient example of a university, in part due to its history, its teaching and scholarship, and in part due to the nature of the colleges that make up the university. Although in many ways atypical in terms of British and other international higher education institutions, people, particularly in the United Kingdom, often rely upon Oxford as a point of comparison for other universities. **Typicality effects** occur when Oxford serves to establish a means of evaluating and assessing another university. (See also **generators, ideals, paragons, social stereotypes, typical examples**.)

sanction The way in which a particular mental **schema** licenses a particular **instantiation**. To illustrate, consider Figure 34.

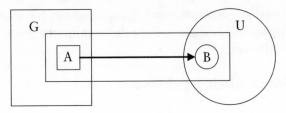

Figure 34. Sanction in Cognitive Grammar

The box labelled G represents the repository of conventional units of language: the **grammar**. The box labelled U represents a particular usage event: an **utterance**. The box labelled A in the grammar represents a **linguistic unit**: a **symbolic assembly**. The circle labelled B represents a specific linguistic element within an utterance. The arrow signals that B instantiates (or 'counts as an instance of') schema A. This means that A sanctions B. (See also **Cognitive Grammar, usage-based model, usage-based thesis**.)

Sapir-Whorf Hypothesis see **linguistic relativity**

scaling In **Blending Theory**, a kind of **compression** in which a **vital relation** holding between **input spaces** (an **outer-space relation**) gives rise to reduced complexity in the **blended space**. Specifically, scaling gives rise to a reduced scale, thereby forming an **inner-space relation**. For instance, the professor who presents the events which have taken place over the 4.6 billion years of evolutionary time in terms of a 24-hour day for the sake of undergraduate students during a lecture on evolution is performing scaling. (See also **syncopation**.)

scanning A notion developed in **Cognitive Grammar**. Relates to how the aspects of a scene are perceived, visually or otherwise, and give rise to a conceptual representation. Two types of scanning are distinguished: **sequential scanning** and **summary scanning** which serve to distinguish between **temporal relations** and **atemporal relations** respectively.

Scene Encoding Hypothesis In **Construction Grammar (2)** the hypothesis that the **prototype** for a particular instance of **constructional polysemy** relates to a recurring scene from everyday experience which is encoded by the **construction (1)**. For instance, while the **ditransitive construction** exhibits **polysemy**, according to *Adele Goldberg*, SUCCESSFUL TRANSFER, as in the following: *Max gave Bella the biscuit*, represents the central or prototypical sense of the ditransitive construction. This follows as this instance of the construction encodes a recurring experiential scene in which an agent causes a recipient to receive some object by way of transfer.

schema A **symbolic assembly** viewed from the perspective of the **usage-based thesis**. (See also **Cognitive Grammar**, **schema-instance organisation**.)

schema induction In **Mental Spaces Theory**, the process whereby knowledge structures such as idealised cognitive models or semantic frames are recruited in order to provide a **mental space** with internal structure. Schema induction is prompted for by linguistic expressions. For instance, in the following utterance: *In the picture the witch is riding the unicorn*, the expression *is riding* prompts for a RIDING frame. This knowledge structure provides roles for RIDER and RIDEE which can be mapped onto the witch and the unicorn respectively, thereby providing the mental space with internal structure.

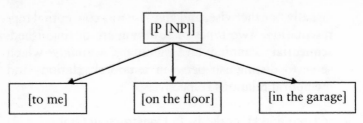

Figure 35. Schema-instance organisation

schema-instance organisation In **Cognitive Grammar**, linguistic units are held to form a structured network of schemas. Schemas are modelled in hierarchical fashion in terms of a more abstract **schema** and more specific **instance**s, as illustrated in Figure 35.

schematic categories The categories which make up the **schematic systems** in the **Conceptual Structuring System Approach**. Each schematic system is made up of several schematic categories which serve to encode different aspects of **schematic meaning**. For instance, the configurational system has a number of schematic categories which include: **plexity, dividedness, boundedness, degree of extension, pattern of distribution, axiality**. These categories structure the scenes encoded by language and the participants that interact within these scenes.

schematic meaning (also **structural meaning, structuring function**) The kind of meaning associated with elements in the **conceptual structuring system** as encoded by **closed class forms**. Meaning of this kind is not rich in nature, and thus contrasts with the meaning associated with elements in the **conceptual content system** as encoded by **open class forms**. Schematic meaning relates to concepts having to do with number, time reference, whether a piece of information is old or new, whether the speaker is providing information or requesting information, and so on. Accordingly, it provides a kind of semantic 'scaffolding' which supports and structures the rich content provided by open class forms and contrasts with **content meaning**. For instance, in the following sentence, schematic meaning is associated with the closed class forms marked in bold: *The movie star kissed the directors*.

Schematic systems In the **Conceptual Structuring System Approach,** the **conceptual structuring system** is based upon a limited number of large-scale schematic systems. These provide the basic organisation of the **cognitive representation** upon which the rich **content meaning** encoded by **open class forms** can be organised and supported. The various schematic systems collaborate to structure a scene that is expressed via language. Each schematic system contributes different structural aspects of the scene, resulting in the overall delineation of the scene's skeletal framework. There are four key schematic systems that have been addressed in detail by *Leonard Talmy* in his work although there are likely to be more. These are the **configurational system**, the **perspectival system**, the **attentional system** and the **force-dynamics system**. (See also **schematic categories.**)

schematisation A special kind of **abstraction**. Results in representations that are much less detailed than the actual utterances that give rise to them. Schematisation results in a **schema**. A schema is achieved by setting aside points of difference between actual structures leaving just the points they have in common. To illustrate, consider the following examples:

1. The kitten is in the box
2. The flower is in the vase
3. The crack is in the vase

Here the lexical item *in* has three slightly different meanings associated with it. These distinct meanings are situated, arising from context. Nevertheless, what is common to each of these uses is the rather abstract notion of enclosure; it is this commonality that establishes the schema for *in*. Moreover, the schema for *in* says very little about the nature of the **figure** and **reference object** that are associated by the **spatial relation** designated by *in*. That is, information stored as part of the schema holds only that the figure and the reference object must exist and that they must have the basic properties that enable enclosure. (See also **usage-based thesis, utterance.**)

scope of predication Relates to that part of a **domain matrix** which is essential for the meaning of a **linguistic unit**. The scope of predication is divided into two constituent entities, the **profile** and the **base**.

search domain That part of a **spatial scene** which is indicated, by linguistic prompts, as the region to be 'searched' in order to locate the **trajector**. For instance, the **utterance**: *near the fire is warmer*, indicates a search domain proximal to the **landmark**, *the fire*, where greatest warmth can be found/experienced.

secondary landmark In a **profiled relationship** when there are two landmarks, the secondary landmark is the participant which has least salience. For instance, in the following example: *Max kicked the ball towards the goal*, there are two landmarks: *the ball* and *the goal*.

The secondary landmark is *the goal*. (See also **landmark, trajector, trajector-landmark organisation**.)

secondary reference object In addition to **figure-ground organisation,** languages often allow more complex partitioning of spatial scenes. This involves segregating the **ground** into two reference objects in order to better locate the **figure**. These are termed the **reference object** and the **secondary reference object**. While the reference object (also known as the primary reference object) is usually explicitly encoded by a lexical item, the secondary reference object need not be, but can instead merely be implied, as in the following: *Big Ben is north of the River Thames*. While *the River Thames* is the primary reference object, the secondary reference object, *the Earth*, is implied by the spatial expression *north of*. In other words, it is only with respect to the concept THE EARTH that we can process the information that one entity can be 'north of' another. The purpose of invoking a secondary reference object is to provide the primary reference object with **axial properties** in order to better locate the figure. This is often necessary when the primary reference object does not possess its own intrinsic asymmetry which can be employed as a **reference frame**. (See also **encompassing secondary reference object** and **external secondary reference object**.)

selection One of the three **parameters of focal adjustment**. Selection determines which aspects of a scene are attended to and relates to the notion of a conceptual **domain (1)**. For instance, in the following examples the lexical item *close* selects for distinct conceptual domains:

1. Max's school is quite close to the   [SPACE]
   Lido

2. It's close to Isabella's birthday   [TIME]
3. That blue is close to the blue of   [COLOUR]
   my dining room carpet
4. Max and Isabella are very close   [EMOTION]

(See also **abstraction (2)**, **construal**, **focal adjustment**, **perspective**.)

selective projection In an **integration network**, the idea that not all the structure present in the **input spaces** is projected to the blended spaces. It is only the information that is subject to **matching** which is required for purposes of local understanding which is projected. Accordingly, the projection of structure from the input spaces to the **blended space** is selective.

Semantic Coherence Principle One of the two principles that facilitate **fusion (1)** in **Construction Grammar (2)**. The Semantic Coherence Principle states that participant roles are matched with argument roles with which they overlap, such that one can be construed as an instance of the other. For example, general categorisation principles enable us to determine that the THIEF participant role of the verb *steal* overlaps sufficiently with the argument role AGENT, because both share semantic properties such as ANIMACY, INTENTION, CAUSATION and so on. (See also **Correspondence Principle**.)

semantic frame A knowledge structure required in order to understand a particular word or related set of words. The semantic frame is central to the theory of **Frame Semantics**. To illustrate, consider the related group of words *buy, sell, pay, spend, cost, charge, tender, change*, and so on. According to Frame Semantics, in order to

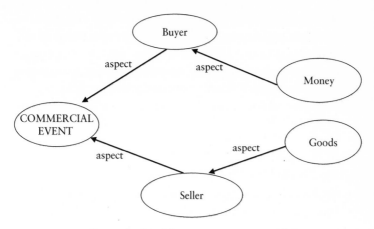

Figure 36. Partial COMMERCIAL EVENT frame

understand these words, we need access to a COMMER-
CIAL EVENT frame, which provides the background
knowledge, based on experience, to which these words
relate. For instance, the COMMERCIAL EVENT frame
includes a number of attributes which must include, at
the very least, BUYER, SELLER, GOODS and MONEY. This
skeletal frame is represented in Figure 36.

Thus a given word foregrounds a particular part of
the semantic frame to which it is relativised, and yet
cannot be understood without the other elements
which make up the frame. One consequence of this is
that a word provides a 'route' through a particular
frame. That is, as words relate to 'slots' in the frame,
they directly relate certain elements within a frame.
This manifests itself in linguistic terms as valence or
argument structure.

Valence concerns the ways in which lexical items
like verbs can be combined with other words to make
grammatical sentences. For example, while *buy* and
pay relate to the actions of the BUYER, *buy* relates to

the interaction between the BUYER and the GOODS, while *pay* relates to the interaction between the BUYER and the SELLER. This knowledge, which is a consequence of the COMMERCIAL EVENT frame, has consequences for grammatical organisation:

1. (a) John bought the car (from the salesperson)
   (b) *John bought the salesperson
2. (a) John paid the salesperson (for the car)
   (b) *John paid the car

The valence of verbs in these utterances (how they combine and with what) is a consequence of how they are related in the COMMERCIAL EVENT semantic frame.

semantic network In **cognitive lexical semantics**, a **linguistic unit** such as a word is treated as being comprised of related senses or lexical concepts. The range of lexical concepts associated with a given word is assumed to form a network of senses which are related by degrees, with some lexical concepts being more central and others more peripheral. Accordingly, word senses are modelled in terms of creating a lattice structure, a semantic network, with a central sense, also known as a **prototype**. (See also **lexical concept, over, radial category**.)

semantic potential In **LCCM Theory**, the nature of **encyclopaedic knowledge** to which an individual **lexical concept** provides potential **access**. That part of a word's semantic potential which is activated is a consequence of linguistic and extralinguistic context. For instance, in the following utterances:

1. France is a region of outstanding beauty
2. France rejected the EU constitution

the semantic contribution of *France* is distinct because of the differential activation of parts of the encyclopaedic knowledge to which *France* provides access. In the example in (1), *France* provides access to that part of the encyclopaedic knowledge relating to France as a geographical landmass of a certain kind. In (2) *France* relates to that portion of the French electorate who voted against the EU constitution. (See also **activation, cognitive model, cognitive model profile.**)

semantic structure The form that **conceptual structure** takes for purposes of being encoded and externalised via language. Semantic structure encompasses the semantic units conventionally associated with linguistic forms. A unit of semantic structure is sometimes referred to as a **lexical concept,** particularly in **LCCM Theory.** (See also **construction (1), semantic pole, symbolic assembly.**)

semantic structure reflects conceptual structure The second of the **guiding principles of cognitive semantics.** Asserts that language refers to concepts in the mind of the speaker rather than, directly, to entities which inhere in an objectively real external world. In other words, **semantic structure** (the meanings conventionally associated with words and other linguistic units) can be equated with **conceptual structure** (that is, concepts). This 'representational' view is directly at odds with the 'denotational' perspective of what cognitive semanticists sometimes refer to as **objectivist semantics.** (See also **cognitive semantics, concept.**)

sensory experience Relates to experience derived from sensory perception (the 'senses') and concerns perceptual data derived from the external world. Concepts that derive from sensory experience include, among others, those relating to the domains of space, motion, temperature and so on. The other category of experience is **subjective experience**. (See also **concept, domain (1)**.)

sentence An abstract entity based on prototypical patterns found in utterances. In other words, a sentence is an idealisation that has determinate properties, often stated in terms of grammatical structure. For example, one definition of (an English) sentence might consist of the formula: S → NP VP. In this formula, 'S' stands for sentence, 'NP' for subject noun phrase and 'VP' for the verb phrase or predicate which provides information about the subject NP. The notion of a sentence, while based on prototypical patterns found in utterances, is not the same as an **utterance**. Much of **formal linguistics** has been concerned with modelling the properties of language that enable us to produce grammatically well-formed sentences. Typically, **cognitive linguistics** places little emphasis on the sentence as a theoretical entity. In contrast, the notion of a usage event or utterance is central to the cognitive perspective.

sequential scanning One type of **scanning**. In sequential scanning, aspects of a scene are scanned in a sequential fashion so that the aspects of the scene are not simultaneously present at any stage of the scanning. This gives rise to a conceptualisation of time as a dynamic process and characterises events. Sequential scanning underpins the conceptual representation that gives rise to **temporal relations**, as encoded, for instance, by verbs. (See also **conceived time**.)

simple atemporal relations A sub-category of **atemporal relations**. A simple atemporal relation designates a state, as encoded by *in* in the following example: *the paper in the bin*. Simple atemporal relations contrast with **complex atemporal relations**.

simple temporal relations A sub-category of **temporal relations**. Simple temporal relations like **complex temporal relations** involve a process, and hence a temporal relation, because they construe scenes that hold over a given span of time. However, a simple temporal relation designates a stable and unchanging state which nevertheless holds or continues through time, as illustrated by the following example: *Max loves chocolate*.

simplex Refers to a **symbolic assembly** which does not contain smaller symbolic units as sub-parts. For example, a simplex symbolic unit such as a morpheme may have a complex semantic or phonological structure, but is 'simple' in terms of symbolic structure as it does not contain smaller symbolic units as sub-parts. The word *dog* and the plural marker *-s* are examples of simplex symbolic assemblies. (See **Cognitive Grammar, complex, linguistic unit.**)

simplex network The simplest kind of **integration network**. A simplex network involves two **input spaces,** one that contains a **frame** with roles and another that contains values. What makes this an integration network is that it gives rise to a **blended space** containing **emergent structure** that is in neither of the input spaces taken individually. Consider the following example: *Max is the son of Angela*. This utterance prompts for an integration network in which there is one input containing a FAMILY frame with roles for MOTHER and SON. The second input contains the values

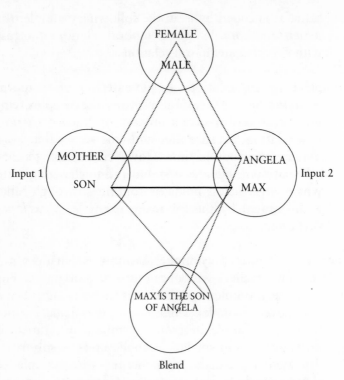

Figure 37. Simplex integration network

JOHN and MARY. The integration network compresses the ROLE-VALUE **outer-space relation** into UNIQUENESS in the blend, so that MAX is the SON and ANGELA the MOTHER, and so that MAX IS ANGELA'S SON. The motivation for the cross-space **connectors** is the **generic space** which contains the elements FEMALE and MALE. These elements identify potential **counterparts** in the input spaces. This integration network is set out diagrammaticaly in Figure 37. (See also **Blending Theory, double-scope network, mirror network, single scope network.**)

simulation The human ability to mentally activate or rehearse perceptual images such as particular sensations or experiences in the absence of the external perceptual stimulus which gives rise to the images. This is achieved, in part, by activating those regions of the brain responsible for processing the sorts of perceptions being simulated. For example, humans can mentally simulate a particular kind of redness, even in the absence of perceiving a red entity. Events can also be simulated, such as the stages involving in filling a car up with petrol, including mentally rehearsing the actions involved in taking the petrol cap off, removing the petrol nozzle from the pump, placing it in the petrol tank, pressing the lever so that the petrol flows into the tank and so on. The ability to simulate can be prompted for by language and is central to some recent theories in cognitive linguistics such as **Blending Theory** and **Embodied Construction Grammar**.

single-scope network A type of **integration network**. In the single scope network both **input spaces** contain a **frame** but each is distinct. Furthermore, only one of the input frames structures the blend. Consider the following example: *Microsoft has finally delivered the knock-out punch to its rival Netscape.* This sentence prompts for an integration network in which there are two input spaces. In one input there are two business rivals, MICROSOFT and NETSCAPE, and Microsoft takes Netscape's market share. In the other input there are two BOXERS, and the first boxer knocks out the second. In the blend, MICROSOFT and NETSCAPE are BOXERS, and MICROSOFT KNOCKS OUT NETSCAPE. What distinguishes this type of network is that only one frame (here the BOXING frame rather than BUSINESS frame) serves to structure the blend. However, the elements

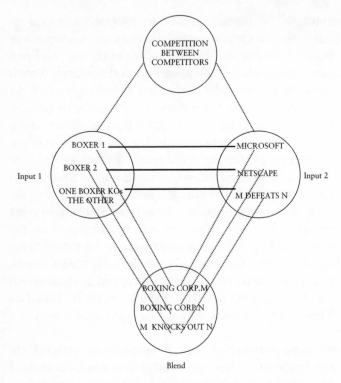

Figure 38. Single scope integration network

from both inputs are projected: roles for BOXERS and values MICROSOFT and NETSCAPE. The integration network for this blend is set out diagrammatically in Figure 38. (See also **Blending Theory, double-scope network, focus input, framing input, metaphoric blend, mirror network, simplex network.**)

situated embodiment A view of **embodied cognition** associated with the work of *Jordan Zlatev*. Relates to the idea that embodiment, as it emerges in semantic structure in language, is embedded or 'situated' within socio-cultural practices. This perspective therefore advocates a synthesis between spatio-physical aspects of embodiment and embodiment as a consequence of the fundamentally social nature of human interaction, practice and function.

social stereotypes A kind of **metonymic ICM**. Social stereotype ICMs are ICMs which emerge from public discussion. For instance, the stereotypical bachelor in our culture is a womaniser who lacks domestic skills. **Typicality effects** can arise if a particular bachelor contrasts with this social stereotype ICM. For instance, an unmarried man with one sexual partner who enjoys staying at home cooking and takes pride in his housework may be judged atypical with respect to the social stereotype for bachelors. (See also **generators, idealised cognitive model, ideals, paragons, salient examples, typical examples.**)

socio-cognitive mechanisms in language acquisition Relates to the view that children bring a battery of socio-cognitive skills to the language acquisition process and is advocated by developmental psycholinguists who take an **emergentism** perspective. These cognitive skills are domain-general: they are not specific to language, but relate to a range of cognitive domains. According to cognitive linguists such as Michael Tomasello these skills facilitate the ability of humans to acquire language. There are two kinds of general cognitive ability that facilitate the acquisition of language: **pattern-finding ability** and **intention-reading ability.**

source domain In **Conceptual Metaphor Theory** the source domain is the **domain (2)** which provides structure by virtue of **metaphor**. This is achieved by **cross-domain mappings** projecting structure from the source domain onto the **target domain** thus establishing a conventional link at the conceptual level. For instance, in the metaphor LOVE IS A JOURNEY, as evidenced by examples such as: *This relationship is going nowhere, Our relationship is stuck in the mud*, JOURNEY is the source domain.

SPACE A fundamental conceptual **domain (1/2)** employed in **Conceptual Metaphor Theory, Cognitive Grammar,** the **Conceptual Structuring System Approach** and **Principled Polysemy**. The domain of SPACE consists of matter which can be continuous or discrete, and locations occupied by matter. The nature of this domain derives from mechanisms central to **perception** which provide **sensory experience** thereby facilitating apprehension of physical aspects of our external physical environment. (See also TIME.)

space builders In **Mental Spaces Theory**, mental spaces are set up by space builders which are linguistic units that either prompt for the construction of a new **mental space** or shift attention back and forth between previously constructed mental spaces. Space builders can be expressions like prepositional phrases (*in 1966, at the shop, in Fred's mind's eye, from their point of view*), adverbs (*really, probably, possibly, theoretically*), connectives (*if . . . then . . .; either . . . or . . .*) and subject-verb combinations that are followed by an embedded sentence (*Fred believes* [*Mary likes bananas*], *Mary hopes . . ., Susan states . . .*). What is special about space builders is that they require the hearer to 'set up' a scenario beyond the 'here and now', whether this scenario reflects past or future reality,

reality in some other location, hypothetical situations, situations that reflect ideas and beliefs, and so on.

spatial relation A relationship, based on spatio-geometric properties, that holds between a **figure** and a **reference object**. For instance, in an utterance such as: *The bike is beside the building,* a spatial relation of proximity and adjacency is designated by the preposition *beside* and what we know about the nature of bikes, buildings and how they are normally located with respect to one another. (See also **figure-ground organisation, reference frame, region**.)

spatial scene A unit of spatial experience as encoded in language. Spatial scenes are configured according to four parameters: a **figure**, also known as the **trajector**; a **reference object**, also known as the **landmark**; a **region**; and potentially a **secondary reference object**, which in combination with the **primary reference object** gives rise to a **reference frame**. For instance, in the spatial scene encoded by the utterance *The bike is next to the school*, *The bike* is the figure and *the school* is the reference object. The region is established by virtue of the combination of the preposition which encodes a **spatial relation** and the reference object and thus serves to encode the location of the figure. The notion of a spatial scene is associated in particular with the **Principled Polysemy** framework as applied to spatial particles.

specific-level metaphor A term coined by *George Lakoff* and *Mark Turner* in their application of **Conceptual Metaphor Theory** to poetic metaphor. Relates to a relatively specific or fine-grained level of metaphoric representation which borrows structure from more schematic or abstract levels of metaphor known as **generic-level metaphor**. The process whereby structure is borrowed by the specific-level metaphor is known as **inheritance**. For instance, the specific-level metaphor LOVE IS A JOURNEY borrows structure from the generic-level metaphors that make up the **Event Structure Metaphor**.

strength One of the factors which governs the **attentional system** in the **conceptual structuring system**. Relates to the relative prominence of referents: whether they are either backgrounded or foregrounded. For instance, in the following example: *The wine merchant sold Edith the champagne*, the focus of attention is on the seller, *the wine merchant*, which illustrates a **focus of attention** pattern. The consequence of this pattern is that *the wine merchant* receives greater attentional strength. (See also **Conceptual Structuring System Approach, mapping, pattern**.)

structural meaning see **schematic meaning**

structuring function see **schematic meaning**

sub-part links One of a number of **inheritance links** between constructions posited in **Construction Grammar (2)**. Involves a type of **inheritance (2)** in which one construction is a proper sub-part of another construction but exists independently. Consider the following example.

1. The French flew Jack to the conference
2. Jack flew

Example (1) is an instance of the **caused motion construction**. Example (2) is an instance of the intransitive motion construction. While (1) lexcially profiles the **argument roles** CAUSE (*The French*), THEME (*Jack*) and GOAL (*the conference*), (2) profiles only the theme (*Jack*). In this sense, the construction illustrated in (2) is a proper sub-part of the construction in (1). Thus the relationship between the two constructions is captured by a sub-part link. (See also **construction (1)**, **profiling**.)

sub-sense (also **micro-sense**) A term coined by *Alan Cruse*. A distinct word meaning that appears to be motivated by the specific situational context in which the word (and the utterance in which the word is embedded) occurs. However, the distinct sense disappears in other contexts. This suggests that sub-senses lack full **autonomy**. The following illustrates a context-specific sub-sense of the lexical item *knife*:

Mother: Haven't you got a knife, Jonny?
Jonny: (*at the table not eating his meat: has penknife in his pocket, but no knife of the appropriate type*) No

Although Jonny does have a knife (a penknife), the context (sitting at the meal table) stipulates that it is not a knife of the appropriate kind, that is it is not a cutlery knife. (See also **facet**.)

subjective construal A form of construal in which there is implicit dependence on the **ground**, and thus the context of the **utterance**, including participants, time of the speech event and so on, is not explicitly mentioned. For instance, the speaker and hearer are usually subjectively construed or 'off stage', and only become objectively construed or 'on stage' when linguistically profiled by expressions such as *I* or *you,* the phenomenon of **objective construal**. (See also **profiling**.)

subjective experience (also **introspective experience**) Experience of this kind is subjective or internal in nature and includes emotions, consciousness and experiences of time such as awareness of duration (including **protracted duration** and **temporal compression**), simultaneity and so on. One of the most fundamental properties of the human **conceptualising capacity** is its tendency to structure concepts or domains relating to introspective experience in terms of concepts that derive from sensory experience. This is evident, for instance, in the phenomenon of conceptual **metaphor**. The other category of experience is **sensory experience**. (See also **concept, domain (1), domain (2)**.)

substantive idioms Idioms of this kind are 'lexically filled', which means that they have fixed lexical items as part of their composition. For example, *kick the mop* does not have the same communicative impact as *kick the bucket* and *spill the champagne* does not have the same communicative impact as *spill the beans*. Both *kick the bucket* and *spill the beans* are substantive idioms because most or all of the substantive or content expressions involved are intrinsic to the idiom. **Idiomatic expressions** of this kind contrast with **formal idioms**. (See also **Construction Grammar (1)**.)

summary scanning One type of **scanning**. In summary scanning, aspects of a scene are scanned cumulatively and are simultaneously present in the conceptual representation. This gives rise to a **gestalt** representation of time as a unified whole and characterises static scenes. Summary scanning underpins the conceptual representation that gives rise to **atemporal relations** as encoded, for instance, by prepositions. (See also **conceived time**.)

superschemas Those elements of **conceptual structure** that are shared both by the **primary target concept** and the **primary source concept** in a given **primary metaphor**. (See also **Superschematic Rule, superschematic structure**.)

Superschematic Rule The requirement within the framework of **Primary Metaphor Theory** that what distinguishes metaphor of any sort from metonymy, idioms and other kinds of figurative expression is that the target and source concepts/domains in a metaphor must share **superschematic structure**. For instance, in the resemblance-based metaphor 'ship of state', in which a nation is conceptualised as a ship on a sea voyage being guided by those making the decisions, both target and source share superschematic structure: they are both bounded entities. (See also **superschemas**.)

superschematic structure A notion developed within **Primary Metaphor Theory**. Relates to the observation that highly schematic elements of **conceptual structure** are shared by the primary target concept and the primary source concept in a **primary metaphor** giving rise to **superschemas**. For instance, in the primary metaphor DIFFICULTY IS HEAVINESS, the superschematic structure that is common to both target: DIFFICULTY, and source: HEAVINESS, is that of a scalar relation. Similarly, what is common to the primary target and source concepts in the primary metaphor ANGER IS HEAT is the superschematic structure of being an unbounded entity. (See also **superschemas, Superschematic Rule.**)

symbolic assembly A **linguistic unit** and the fundamental unit of grammar in *Ronald Langacker's* theory of **Cognitive Grammar**. The symbolic assembly has two poles: a semantic pole (its meaning) and a phonological pole (its sound or form). Symbolic units can be **simplex** or **complex** in terms of their symbolic structure.

symbolic thesis One of the two **guiding principles of cognitive approaches to grammar**. The symbolic thesis holds that the fundamental unit of grammar is a form-meaning pairing, a **linguistic unit** (called a **symbolic assembly** in *Langacker's* **Cognitive Grammar** or a **construction (1)** in **construction grammars**). This is at odds with the 'words and rules' approach to grammar adopted in **formal linguistics**.

By adopting the **symbolic thesis, cognitive approaches to grammar** are not restricted to investigating aspects of grammatical structure independently of meaning, as is often the case in formal linguistics. Instead, cognitive approaches to grammar encompass the entire inventory of linguistic units defined as form-meaning pairings. These run the gamut from skeletal syntactic configurations such as the ditransitive construction (expressed in *John baked Mary a cake*) to idioms (like *kick the bucket*), to bound morphemes like the *-er* suffix, to words. This entails that the **modular approach** towards language and the mind cannot be meaningfully upheld within **cognitive linguistics** where the boundary between **cognitive semantics** and cognitive approaches to grammar is less clearly defined. Instead, meaning and grammar are seen as mutually interdependent and complementary. (See also **usage-based thesis.**)

symbolic unit see **linguistic unit**

syncopation In **Blending Theory**, a kind of **compression** in which a **vital relation** holding between **input spaces** (an **outer-space relation**) gives rise to reduced complexity in the **blended space**, thereby giving rise to an **inner-space relation**. Specifically, syncopation reduces the number of events in a temporal 'string'. For example, a pictorial 'time-line' used to represent evolutionary development, for instance, can select just a few notable events in evolution, such as the emergence and extinction of the dinosaurs, followed by the emergence of primates, and then hominids, and then homo sapiens; this represents compression by syncopation. (See also **scaling**.)

$\boxed{\text{T}}$

target (1) The entity in conceptual **metonymy** which is highlighted or accessed by virtue of a second entity known as a **vehicle**. A target is typically not encoded linguistically in linguistic manifestations of metonymy. For instance, in the following utterance: *Downing Street refused comment*, the target is Prime Minister. Downing Street is the official residence of the British Prime Minister which facilitates metonymic access to Prime Minister. This particular metonymy can be stated employing the formula PLACE FOR PERSON or PLACE FOR INSTITUTION in which the target comes second in the formula. (See also **Domain Highlighting Model**.)

target (2) The entity which is identified in an **utterance** by virtue of invoking a particular **reference point**. To illustrate, consider the following example: *You know that* *girl who works part-time in the Dean's office? Well, her room-mate is having an affair with a much older married man from out of town.* In this example the 'room-mate' is the target, the entity invoked by virtue of the 'girl who works in the Dean's office' which serves as a reference point. (See also **dominion**.)

target domain In **Conceptual Metaphor Theory** the target domain is the **domain (2)** being structured by virtue of **metaphor**. This is achieved due to **cross-domain mappings** projecting structure from the **source domain** onto the target domain thus establishing a conventional link at the conceptual level. For instance, in the metaphor LOVE IS A JOURNEY, as evidenced by examples such as: *This relationship is going nowhere, Our relationship is stuck in the mud*, LOVE is the target domain.

target domain override A constraint on the **Invariance Principle**. Serves to ensure that a **metaphoric entailment** that is incompatible with the **target domain** will fail to map. That is, the target domain can override a metaphoric entailment projected from the **source domain** in a way that preserves the cognitive topology (**conceptual structure**) of the target domain. To illustrate, consider the examples below which relate to the **metaphor** CAUSATION IS TRANSFER (OF AN OBJECT):

1. She gave him a headache   STATE
2. She gave him a kiss   EVENT

While the source domain for both of these examples is TRANSFER, the first example relates to a STATE and the second to an EVENT. The source domain TRANSFER entails that the recipient is in possession of the transferred entity. However, while this entailment is in keeping with STATES, because they are temporally unbounded, the same entailment is incompatible with EVENTS, because they are temporally bounded and cannot therefore 'stretch' across time. This is illustrated below:

3. She gave him a headache and he still
   has it   STATE
4. *She gave him a kiss and he still has it   EVENT

Thus, in the case of the example in (4), the domain relating to events overrides the projection of the entailment of continued possession from the source domain as such an entailment is incompatible with this particular target.

temporal compression The phenomenologically real experience in which time 'feels' as if it is proceeding 'more slowly' than usual and is most often associated with our experience of routine behaviours which we carry out effortlessly without much attention to the task at hand. In **cognitive linguistics** this notion has been studied in detail by *Vyvyan Evans*. Evidence that temporal compression is encoded in language comes from examples such as the following: *The time has sped/whizzed by; Where has the time gone? Time flies when you're having fun.* (See also **protracted duration**.)

temporal relations (also **process**) A sub-category of the larger category **relational predication**. Temporal relations are processes which are encoded by verbs and which are accessed via **sequential scanning**. Temporal relations can be divided into two types: **simple temporal relations** and **complex temporal relations**. (See also **atemporal relations, conceived time, processing time, summary scanning**.)

LATER   EARLIER

Figure 39. The temporal sequence model

temporal sequence model The term given to the **time-based cognitive model for time** in English by *Vyvyan Evans*. This model relates to the concepts EARLIER and LATER. Unlike the moving ego and moving time cognitive models, this cognitive model does not involve an ego (and thus the subjective experience of now). Instead, a temporal event is understood relative to another earlier or later temporal event. The model is illustrated in Figure 39. Directionality is signalled by the arrow. Earlier events (events are represented by the small circles) are understood as being located in front of later events.

To illustrate the temporal sequence model consider the following linguistic examples:

1. Monday precedes/comes before Tuesday
2. Tuesday follows/comes after Monday

In these sentences, LATER follows EARLIER: the earlier event, Monday, is understood as being located in front of the later event, Tuesday. In other words, it is relative to Tuesday, rather than an ego (the subjective experience of now), that Monday is EARLIER. (See also **moving ego model, moving time model.**)

Thesis of Embodied Cognition see **Embodied Cognition**

thing In **Cognitive Grammar,** a technical term for any given region of a conceptual **domain (1)** encoded by a noun. (See also **nominal predication.**)

thinking for speaking A term coined by *Dan Slobin*. Captures the idea that a particular language forces its speakers to pay attention to certain aspects of scenes of experience for purposes of semantic and grammatical encoding in the native language in question. In other words, language is one form that **cognition** takes, and the ideas we wish to express must conform to the linguistic conventions of a given language.

TIME An important conceptual **domain** assumed by **Conceptual Metaphor Theory, Cognitive Grammar,** the **Conceptual Structuring System Approach** as well as other theoretical approaches and perspectives in **cognitive linguistics.**

The domain of TIME consists of actions and events which exhibit the properties of chronology (or progression) and duration. The nature and structure of this domain relates to and derives from neurological and cognitive aspects of **subjective experience** including **protracted duration** and **temporal compression.** The cognitive linguistics of TIME have been studied most extensively by *Vyvyan Evans*. He argues that the domain of TIME is encoded in language at two levels of representation: the **lexical concept** and the **cognitive model.**

In **Cognitive Grammar** TIME, which is a **basic domain,** is divided into **conceived time** and **processing time** and is important for, among other things, the distinction between **temporal relations** and **atemporal relations.**

In the **Conceptual Structuring System Approach,** the domains of TIME and SPACE are held to constitute **homologous categories** and can thus exhibit **conceptual alternativity.** (See also **ego-based cognitive model for time, time-based cognitive model for time.**)

time-based cognitive model for time A temporal **reference frame** which serves to 'locate' events by virtue of their relationship to other temporal events. A central inference associated with this **cognitive model** is the distinction between earlier and later events. The specific time-based cognitive model in English is known as the **temporal sequence model**. (See also **ego-based cognitive model for time, moving ego model, moving time model**.)

TR see **trajector**

trajector (also **TR**) The focal, or most prominent, participant in a **profiled relationship**. (See also **multiplex trajector, over, trajector-landmark organisation**.)

trajector-landmark organisation A notion developed in **Cognitive Grammar**. Relates to the relative prominence of participants in a linguistically encoded scene and reflects the more general perceptual phenomenon of **figure-ground organisation**. *Ronald Langacker* argues that the grammatical functions subject and object are reflections of trajector-landmark organisation. Langacker calls the semantic pole of the **symbolic assembly** that fulfils the subject function the **trajector**, which reflects the observation that the prototypical subject is dynamic. The semantic pole of the symbolic assembly that fulfils the object function is called the **landmark**. This reflects the observation that the prototypical object is stationary or inert, as evidenced by an example such as the following: *The car passed the garage*. (See also **action chain**.)

trajector-landmark reversal A grammatical phenomenon in which the **trajector** and **landmark** in a **profiled**

relationship are reversed. For instance, active and passive constructions exhibit trajector-landmark reversal in that the agent constitutes the trajector in an active construction while the patient is the landmark. In a passive construction the patient is construed as the trajector and the agent is demoted to the backgrounded landmark.

typical examples A kind of **metonymic ICM**. Typicality ICMs arise from a typical example of a particular category. For instance, in some cultures ROBIN and SPARROW are typical members of the category BIRD. This is because in some parts of the world these birds are very common. In this respect, our environment has consequences for what we judge as good examples of a category. Furthermore, we may evaluate a member of the category BIRD with respect to a typical example. In this way, **typicality effects** arise when the typical example stands for the entire category. (See also **generators, ideals, paragons, salient examples, social stereotypes.**)

typicality effects Relates to the phenomenon whereby a particular instance or exemplar is judged as being more or less representative of a given category. Typicality effects are held, in **Prototype Theory**, to result from the **prototype structure** of human categories and are measurable by **goodness-of-example ratings**. For instance, while a robin, for many people, might be judged to be a representative example of the category BIRD, ostrich would be judged to be not very representative and thus non-typical. These differential judgements in terms of representativeness are what are known as typicality effects. (See also **prototype.**)

U

unidirectionality The view in **Conceptual Metaphor Theory** that conceptual metaphors serve to map structure from a **source domain** to a **target domain** but not vice versa. For example, while LOVE is conceptualised in terms of JOURNEYS, we cannot conventionally structure JOURNEYS in terms of LOVE: travellers are not conventionally described as 'lovers' or car crashes in terms of 'heartbreak' and so on. Hence there is a general constraint on the **cross-domain mappings** that underpin conceptual **metaphor** which holds that the mappings are unidirectional.

unification In **Primary Metaphor Theory,** this is the process whereby two or more primary metaphors combine so as to give rise to a **compound metaphor**. For instance, *Joseph Grady*, the architect of Primary Metaphor Theory, argues that the metaphor THEORIES ARE BUILDINGS is a compound metaphor which derives from the unification of the primary metaphors PERSISTING IS REMAINING ERECT and ORGANISATION IS PHYSICAL STRUCTURE. This is set out diagrammatically in Figure 40.

usage event see **utterance**.

usage-based model A model of language which adopts the **usage-based thesis**. A salient example of such a model is the theory of **Cognitive Grammar**.

usage-based thesis One of the two **guiding principles of cognitive approaches to grammar**. The usage-based thesis holds that the mental grammar of the **language user** (his or her knowledge of language) is formed by the **abstraction** of symbolic units from situated

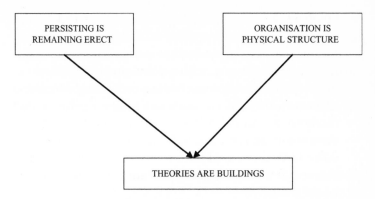

Figure 40. Unification in Primary Metaphor Theory

instances of language use: an **utterance**. An important consequence of adopting the usage-based thesis is that there is no principled distinction between knowledge of language and use of language (competence and performance in Generative Grammar terms), since knowledge of language *is* knowledge of how language is used. The usage-based thesis is central not just to **cognitive approaches to grammar** but approaches to both language change and language acquisition which take a cognitive linguistic perspective, as developed, for instance, by *Michael Tomasello* and *William Croft*.

utterance (also **usage event**) A situated instance of language use which is culturally and contextually embedded and represents an instance of linguistic behaviour on the part of a **language user**.

An utterance has a unit-like status in that it represents the expression of a coherent idea, making (at least partial) use of the **conventions** of the language. In other words, an utterance is a somewhat discrete entity. Nevertheless, an utterance is not an absolutely discrete or precisely identifiable unit. This is because utterances involve grammatical forms (for example, word order), semantic structures (patterns of meaning), speech sounds, patterns of intonation (for example, pitch contours), slight pauses, and accelerations and decelerations. While these properties converge on discreteness and unity, they do not co-occur in fixed patterns and therefore do not provide a set of criteria for collectively identifying an utterance. In this respect, utterances differ from the related notion of **sentence**. In particular, they exhibit **graded grammaticality**. (See also **usage-based thesis**).

utterance schema A term coined by the developmental psychologist *Michael Tomasello*. Relates to an early multi-word utterance in first language acquisition which exhibits functional asymmetry. That is, the expressions contain a relatively stable element with 'slots' that can be filled by other lexical items. Thus early multi-word utterances, rather than containing two or more words of equal status, tend to be 'built' around a functionally more salient and stable word. Some examples of attested utterance schemas include: *Here's the X, I wanna X, More X, It's a X, There's a X, Put X here, Throw X, X gone, X here*. The obligatory element in an utterance schema is known as the 'pivot'.

Like a **holophrase**, an utterance schema reflects the communicative intention of an equivalent adult utterance, but represents the acquisition of more schematic knowledge, allowing a wider range of lexical items to fill the slots. (See also **verb-island construction**.)

Utterance Selection Theory A usage-based theory of language change developed by *William Croft*. This theory views language use as the interface that mediates between the **conventions** of a language (those aspects of use that make a language stable) and mechanisms that result in deviation from convention resulting in language change. For linguistic conventions to change someone must break a convention and this **innovation** must then undergo **propagation**: the change spreads through the linguistic community and becomes established as a new convention. Language change is viewed as a consequence of selectional pressures exerted on linguistic conventions, because language is a system in use that changes as a response to the new uses to which it is put. Borrowing ideas from evolutionary theory Croft argues that innovations which are successful, in the sense of being selected by language users by virtue of being replicated, give rise to propagation and thus result in language change.

As this theory subscribes to the **usage-based thesis**, the key construct in the Theory of Utterance Selection is the **utterance**. The elements of an utterance that are reproduced by language users are referred to as **replicators**. The elements of language that are realised in an utterance and that can therefore count as replicators include words, morphemes and grammatical constructions. Croft calls these linguistic replicators **linguemes**.

V

valence see **argument structure**

variable embodiment The idea that different organisms have different kinds of experiences due to the nature of their embodiment. (See also **embodied cognition, embodied experience, embodiment**.)

Vehicle The entity in conceptual **metonymy** which serves to provide **access** to or to highlight a second entity known as a **target**. A vehicle is typically encoded linguistically. For instance, in the following utterance: *Downing Street refused comment*, the vehicle is Downing Street, the official London residence of the Prime Minister. The vehicle facilitates metonymic access to Prime Minister. This particular metonymy can be stated employing the formula PLACE FOR PERSON or PLACE FOR INSTITUTION in which the vehicle comes first in the formula. (See also **Domain Highlighting Model**.)

verb argument constructions The set of constructions associated with verbal **argument structure** studied by *Adele Goldberg* in developing her theory of **Construction Grammar (2)**. These include the **caused motion construction, the ditransitive construction** and the **resultative construction**. (See also **construction (1)**.)

verb-island construction A type of **utterance schema**. As most utterance schemas appear to revolve around verb-like elements, *Michael Tomasello* labels these units verb-island constructions.

viewpoint space The **mental space** from which the discourse is currently being viewed and from which other spaces in a **mental spaces lattice** are currently being built. (See also **base space, event space, focus space, Mental Spaces Theory**.)

vital relations In an **integration network**, vital relations are the **connectors** that serve to identify **counterparts** within and across mental spaces. *Gilles Fauconnier* and *Mark Turner* argue that there is a relatively small set of vital relations which recur frequently in conceptual

Table 12. Vital relations

Outer-space vital relation	Inner-space vital relation (compression)
TIME	SCALED TIME
	SYNCOPATED TIME
SPACE	SCALED SPACE
	SYNCOPATED SPACE
REPRESENTATION	UNIQUENESS
CHANGE	UNIQUENESS
ROLE-VALUE	UNIQUENESS
ANALOGY	IDENTITY
	CATEGORY
DISANALOGY	CHANGE
	UNIQUENESS
PART-WHOLE	UNIQUENESS
CAUSE-EFFECT (bundled with TIME and CHANGE)	SCALED TIME UNIQUENESS
CAUSE-EFFECT	PROPERTY

integration. It is precisely the frequency with which these connectors occur that licenses the application of the term 'vital' to describe them.

The importance of vital relations is that conceptual integration proceeds by virtue of **compression** of a given vital relation holding between counterparts in distinct **input spaces,** resulting in a compressed vital relation which is projected to the **blended space.** A vital relation which connects counterparts across input spaces is known as an **outer-space relation.** The compressed vital relation that occurs in the blended space is known as an **inner-space relation.** Table 12 provides some examples of outer-space vital relations and their compression into inner-space vital relations. (See also **Blending Theory, scaling, syncopation.**)

W

What's X doing Y? construction (also **WXDY construction**) An idiomatic expression studied by *Paul Kay* and *Charles Fillmore* in support of their theory of **Construction Grammar (1)**. Like the **let alone construction**, the What's X doing Y? construction is a productive **formal idiom** that has identifiable syntactic, semantic and pragmatic properties. What is 'special' about the WXDY construction is the incongruity judgement it gives rise to. This construction is illustrated by the examples below.

1. What's [$_x$ John] doing [$_y$ kissing that woman]?
2. What are [$_x$ these dishes] doing [$_y$ in the sink]?
3. What's that [$_x$ man] doing [$_y$ with my necktie on]?
4. What's [$_x$ Mike] doing [$_y$ with that hosepipe]?
5. What is [$_x$ Jane] doing [$_y$ covered in spaghetti]?
6. What is [$_x$ Mary] doing [$_y$ naked]?

As these examples illustrate, the construction lends itself to a wide range of specific examples. The Y part of the construction is particularly flexible and can be headed by various categories including participial verb forms (*kissing, covered*), prepositions (*in, with, without*) or adjectives (*naked*). (See also **idiomatic expressions**.)

window of attention One of the kinds of **pattern** which serve to govern the distribution of attention in the **attentional system**. The window of attention pattern involves the explicit mention of some part or parts of an event ('windowing'), while other parts may be omitted ('gapping'). The windowing pattern differs from the **focus of attention** pattern which focuses attention on participants. For instance, a path of motion consists of a beginning, a middle and an end.

In the following examples, the whole path of motion is windowed in (1), whereas in the examples in (2–4) only the initial, medial or final portion of the path is windowed, respectively:

1. The champagne cork shot out of the bottle, through the air and into Jane's eye
2. The champagne cork shot out of the bottle [initial]
3. The champagne cork shot through the air [medial]
4. The champagne cork shot into Jane's eye [final]

(See also **conceptual structuring system, Conceptual Structuring System Approach.**)

WXDY construction see **What's X doing Y? construction**

XYZ construction A grammatical **construction (1)** specialised for prompting for **conceptual integration** studied in detail by *Mark Turner*. Some examples of this construction include the following:

1. Money is the root of all evil
2. Vanity is the quicksand of beauty
3. Necessity is the mother of invention
4. Death is the mother of beauty
5. Children are the riches of poor men

These examples all share a form first noted by Aristotle in the *Poetics*. The form consists of three elements, x, y and z. These are all noun phrases. Two of the elements, y and z, form a possessive construction (bracketed) connected by the preposition 'of'. The purpose of the construction is to propose a particular perspective according to which x should be viewed, as indicated below:

6. <u>Children</u> are [<u>the riches</u> of <u>poor men</u>]
   x   Y   z

In (6), we are asked to view children as the riches of poor men, which results in a number of positive inferences relating to the 'value' of children. In addition to the elements x, y and z, the construction prompts for a fourth element, w. In order to understand children (x) in terms of riches (y) we are prompted to construct a conceptual relation between children (x) and poor men (z) and a parallel relation holding between riches (y) and those who possess riches, namely rich men. This is the missing element (w), which is a necessary component to the interpretation of this construction: in the absence of a y–w (RICHES–RICH MEN) relationship parallel to the x–z (CHILDREN–POOR MEN) relationship, there is no basis for viewing children (x) and riches (y) as counterparts. This idea is illustrated in (7).

7. (a) CHILDREN ↔ POOR MEN
         x   z
   (b) RICHES ↔ RICH MEN
         Y   W

According to **Blending Theory**, 'children/poor men' and 'riches/rich men' each inhabit distinct **input spaces**. The XYZ construction prompts for **conceptual integration** which serves to give rise to the analogy in terms of which children are conceptualised in terms of the riches of poor men. This is the **emergent structure**.

Annotated Further Reading

Below you will find an annotated listing of books that will allow you to discover more about cognitive linguistics. The selection of books has been divided into four sections:

1. textbooks;
2. works of reference;
3. core readings in cognitive semantics;
4. core readings in cognitive approaches to grammar.

Textbooks

Croft, William and D. Alan Cruse (2004) *Cognitive Linguistics*. Cambridge: Cambridge University Press.

A recent introduction to cognitive linguistics. Particularly good coverage of lexical semantics and constructional approaches to grammar.

Evans, Vyvyan and Melanie Green (2006) *Cognitive Linguistics: An Introduction*. Mahwah, NJ and Edinburgh: Lawrence Erlbaum Associates/Edinburgh University Press.

The most comprehensive general introduction to the field. Each chapter provides a detailed annotated reading list and exercises. Also includes chapters which compare cognitive linguistic theories with other theoretical frameworks.

Kövecses, Zoltán (2002) *Metaphor: A Practical Introduction*. Oxford: Oxford University Press.
An accessible introduction to the key ideas in Conceptual Metaphor Theory.

Lee, David (2001) *Cognitive Linguistics: An Introduction*. Oxford: Oxford University Press.
An accessible general introduction, focusing on general ideas rather than detail. The selection of topics covered, is, nevertheless, a little uneven.

Taylor, John (2002) *Cognitive Grammar*. Oxford: Oxford University Press.
An excellent textbook introduction to Langacker's theory.

Taylor, John (2003) *Linguistic Categorization*, 3rd edn. Oxford: Oxford University Press.
Provides a highly accessible account of cognitive linguistic approaches to typicality effects and fuzzy categories as manifested in language.

Ungerer, Friedrich and Hans-Jorg Schmid (2006) *Introduction to Cognitive Linguistics*, 2nd edn. London: Longman.
Very clear explanations of the areas presented, particularly on prototype and basic level objects research. However, the coverage is rather one-sided focusing primarily on (older traditions in) cognitive semantics.

Works of reference

Cuyckens, Hubert, René Dirven and John Taylor (2003) *Cognitive Approaches to Lexical Semantics*. Berlin: Mouton de Gruyter.

An excellent representative selection of original articles relating to contemporary approaches to cognitive lexical semantics.

Dirven, René and Ralf Pörings (2002) *Metaphor and Metonymy in Comparison and Contrast*. Berlin: Mouton de Gruyter.
A collection reproducing seminal and influential articles relating to conceptual metaphor and metonymy.

Evans, Vyvyan, Benjamin Bergen and Jörg Zinken (2007) *The Cognitive Linguistics Reader*. London: Equinox.
The largest single-volume collection of readings in cognitive linguistics and a significant work of reference. Contains twenty-eight articles by leading figures in cognitive linguistics including a major review article of the cognitive linguistics enterprise written by the *Reader's* editors.

Fauconnier, Gilles and Eve Sweetser (1996) *Spaces, Worlds and Grammar*. Chicago: University of Chicago Press.
An edited volume consisting of original articles which address various semantic and grammatical issues making use of Fauconnier's theory of mental spaces.

Geeraerts, Dirk (2006) *Cognitive Linguistics: Basic Readings*. Berlin: Mouton de Gruyter.
A collection of twelve seminal articles by leading figures in cognitive linguistics.

Geeraerts, Dirk and Hubert Cuyckens (In press) *Oxford Handbook of Cognitive Linguistics*. Oxford: Oxford University Press.
A major reference work containing original encyclopaedia-like articles by leading experts.

Gonzalez-Marquez, Monica, Irene Mittelberg, Seana Coulson and Michael Spivey (eds) (2006) *Empirical Methods in Cognitive Linguistics*. Amsterdam, NJ: John Benjamins.
A recent edited volume comprising original articles by prominent cognitive linguists and psychologists. The collection both makes the case for empirical methods in cognitive linguistics and represents the state of the art.

Gries, Stefan Th. and Anatol Stefanowitsch (eds) (2006) *Corpora in Cognitive Linguistics*. Berlin: Mouton de Gruyter.
An important contribution that makes the case for the use of empirical corpus-based linguistics in cognitive linguistic theorising.

Hampe, Beate (2005) *From Perception to Meaning: Image Schemas in Cognitive Linguistics*. Berlin: Mouton de Gruyter.
An edited collection of papers by leading scholars presenting a range of often conflicting positions on the nature of image schemas.

Janssen, Theo and Gisela Redeker (1999) *Cognitive Linguistics: Foundations, Scope and Methodology*. Berlin: Mouton de Gruyter.
An edited volume containing original articles by a selection of leading cognitive linguists. The articles address the theoretical and empirical basis of cognitive linguistics and cognitive linguistic theories.

Östman, Jan Ola and Mirjam Fried (2005) *Construction Grammars: Cognitive Grounding and Theoretical Extensions*. Amsterdam, NJ: John Benjamins.

An edited collection of original papers addressing theoretical and methodological issues relating to constructional approaches to grammar.

Core readings in cognitive semantics

Coulson, Seana (2000) *Semantic Leaps: Frame-Shifting and Conceptual Blending in Meaning Construction.* Cambridge: Cambridge University Press.
An important study on the role of conceptual blending in language processing and comprehension.

Croft, William (2000) *Explaining Language Change: An Evolutionary Perspective.* London: Longman.
A seminal work in which Croft presents a usage-based theory of language change which applies insights from the generalised theory of natural selection to language.

Dancygier, Barbara and Eve Sweetser (2005) *Mental Spaces in Grammar: Conditional Constructions.* Cambridge: Cambridge University Press.
Presents a theoretical account of conditional constructions using the framework of Mental Spaces Theory.

Evans, Vyvyan (2004) *The Structure of Time: Language, Meaning and Temporal Cognition.* Amsterdam, NJ: John Benjamins.
Investigates the relationship between lexical and conceptual structure in the domain of time. The only book-length treatment of temporal cognition from the perspective of cognitive linguistics. Also represents a precursor to the development of LCCM Theory.

Fauconnier, Gilles (1994) *Mental Spaces.* Cambridge: Cambridge University Press.

This is a revised edition of Fauconnier's classic book, first published in English in 1985. Presents a groundbreaking theory of semantic reference, successfully resolving many semantic phenomena which had bedevilled formal approaches.

Fauconnier, Gilles (1997) *Mappings in Thought and Language*. Cambridge: Cambridge University Press.
In this volume Fauconnier updates and extends his theory of mental spaces. He also introduces his collaborative work with Mark Turner on Conceptual Blending Theory.

Fauconnier, Gilles and Mark Turner (2002) *The Way We Think: Conceptual Blending and the Mind's Hidden Complexities*. New York: Basic Books.
The definitive introduction to conceptual blending by the two architects of the theory. Highly accessible.

Feldman, Jerome (2006) *From Molecule to Metaphor: A Neural Theory of Language*. Cambridge, MA: MIT Press.
An extremely accessible introduction to the Neural Theory of Language project associated with cognitive linguists and cognitive scientists at the University of California, Berkeley.

Gibbs, Raymond (1994) *The Poetics of Mind*. Cambridge: Cambridge University Press.
Presents psycholinguistic evidence for the conceptual basis of figurative language phenomena such as metaphor.

Johnson, Mark (1987) *The Body in the Mind: The Bodily Basis of Meaning, Imagination and Reason*. Chicago: Chicago University Press.

One of the classic texts in cognitive linguistics. Provides the first detailed treatment of image schemas.

Lakoff, George (1987) *Women, Fire and Dangerous Things: What Categories Reveal About the Mind.* Chicago: University of Chicago Press.
One of the classic texts in cognitive linguistics. Lakoff makes the case for a novel theory of idealised cognitive models in order to account for recent findings in human categorisation. Also provides a philosophical framework for research in cognitive linguistics which remains influential.

Lakoff, George and Mark Johnson (1999) *Philosophy in the Flesh: The Embodied Mind and Its Challenge to Western Thought.* New York: Basic Books.
An updated account of Lakoff and Johnson's seminal ideas on conceptual metaphors and the notion of embodied cognition.

Lakoff, George and Mark Johnson (2003) *Metaphors We Live By*, 2nd revised edn. Chicago: University of Chicago Press.
This classic introduction to Conceptual Metaphor Theory was originally published in 1980. The second edition features a new afterword detailing some of the more recent insights and developments in metaphor research.

Palmer, Gary (1996) *Toward a Theory of Cultural Linguistics.* Austin, TX: University of Texas Press.
In this book Palmer makes a compelling case for applying cognitive linguistics to cultural aspects of language, arguing for a theory of cultural linguistics.

Sweetser, Eve (1990) *From Etymology to Pragmatics: Metaphorical and Cultural Aspects of Semantic Structure.* Cambridge: Cambridge University Press.
Another highly influential and now classic text in cognitive linguistics. Sweetser uses ideas from Conceptual Metaphor Theory and Image Schema Theory in order to account for semantic aspects of grammatical change.

Talmy, Leonard (2000) *Toward a Cognitive Semantics*, Vols I and II. Cambridge, MA: MIT Press.
Brings together, and updates, Talmy's classic papers in which he explores how language encodes various aspects of conceptual structure including space, force-dynamics and motion.

Tyler, Andrea and Vyvyan Evans (2003) *The Semantics of English Prepositions: Spatial Scenes, Embodied Experience and Cognition.* Cambridge: Cambridge University Press.
The first book-length treatment of the Principled Polysemy approach to lexical representation. Also represents the most detailed cognitive linguistic study of English spatial relations. The book makes the case for the experiential basis of prepositional meanings and their extensions.

Core readings in cognitive approaches to grammar
Croft, William (2002) *Radical Construction Grammar.* Oxford: Oxford University Press.
Introduces and makes the case for a Radical Construction Grammar.

Dabrowska, Ewa (2004) *Language, Mind and Brain: Some Psychological and Neurological Constraints on Grammar.* Edinburgh: Edinburgh University Press.

An excellent and highly accessible overview and review of the cognitive linguistic position with respect to key issues in psycholinguistics, including language acquisition, brain lateralisation and modularity. Also includes a review of cognitive linguistic criticisms of Chomsky's Universal Grammar hypothesis.

Goldberg, Adele (1995) *Constructions: A Construction Grammar Approach to Verbal Argument Structure.* Chicago: University of Chicago Press.
A classic. Makes a compelling case for a constructional approach to grammar employing verbal argument constructions as a test case.

Goldberg, Adele (2006) *Constructions at Work: The Nature of Generalization in Language.* Oxford: Oxford University Press.
An updated constructional account. Also includes new findings on the way children acquire constructions.

Langacker, Ronald (1987/1991) *Foundations of Cognitive Grammar*, Vols I and II. Stanford, CA: Stanford University Press.
Volume I of Langacker's two-volume edifice lays out the theoretical assumptions of his theory of Cognitive Grammar. Volume II applies the theoretical architecture to a range of grammatical phenomena.

Tomasello, M. (2003) *Constructing a Language: A Usage-Based Theory of Language Acquisition.* Cambridge, MA: Harvard University Press.
An important recent synthesis of empirical findings relating to first language acquisition. Presents the case for a usage-based perspective on language acquisition.

Authors Mentioned

Below you will find a list of researchers mentioned in the Glossary, followed by a listing of some of the areas of research undertaken by each researcher.

Jens Allwood
Cognitive lexical semantics, meaning-construction

Antonio Barcelona
Metaphor, metonymy

Lawrence Barsalou
Framing, knowledege representation, perceptual simulation

Elizabeth Bates
Developmental psycholinguistics, emergentism

Benjamin Bergen
Construction Grammar, Embodied Construction Grammar

Claudia Brugman
Cognitive lexical semantics, over

Nancy Chang
First language acquisition, Embodied Construction
Grammar

Seana Coulson
Blending Theory, language comprehension, language
processing, Mental Spaces Theory

William Croft
Construction Grammar, Domain Highlighting Model,
language change, linguistic typology, Radical
Construction Grammar, Utterance Selection Theory

D. Alan Cruse
Cognitive lexical semantics

Hubert Cuyckens
Cognitive lexical semantics, prepositions

Barbara Dancygier
Blending Theory, conditional constructions, Mental
Spaces Theory

Paul Deane
Cognitive lexical semantics, prepositions

Merlin Donald
Cognitive development, evolutionary psychology,
mimesis

Vyvyan Evans
Cognitive lexical semantics, metaphor, meaning-
construction, LCCM Theory, prepositions, Principled
Polysemy, temporal representation

Gilles Fauconnier
Blending Theory, Mental Spaces Theory

Jerome Feldman
Cognitive science, Neural Theory of Language

Charles Fillmore
Construction Grammar, Frame Semantics

Dirk Geeraerts
Cognitive lexical semantics, historical lexicology

Raymond Gibbs
Embodied cognition, empirical approaches to cognitive
linguistics, metaphor, metonymy

Adele Goldberg
Construction Grammar, first language acquisition

Louis Goossens
Metaphor, metonymy

Joseph Grady
Metaphor, Primary Metaphor Theory

Anette Herskovits
Cognitive lexical semantics, prepositions

Paul Hopper
Construction Grammar, discourse analysis, Emergent
Grammar, grammaticalisation

Ray Jackendoff
Conceptual semantics, constuctional approaches to
grammar

Mark Johnson
Conceptual Metaphor Theory, image schemas, metaphor, applications of cognitive semantics to philosophy

Paul Kay
Colour categorisation, Construction Grammar

Zoltán Kövecses
Conceptual Metaphor Theory, metaphor, metonymy, cultural linguistics

Tania Kuteva
Distributed spatial semantics, grammaticalisation

George Lakoff
Categorisation, cognitive lexical semantics, Conceptual Metaphor Theory, Construction Grammar, framing, metaphor, Neural Theory of Language, application of cognitive semantics to politics

Ronald Langacker
Cognitive Grammar

John Lucy
Linguistic relativity

Jean Mandler
Cognitive development, image schemas, knowledge representation, language development

Laura Michaelis
Construction Grammar, Embodied Construction Grammar

Rafael Núñez
Cognitive science, temporal representation in language and gesture, application of cognitive semantics to mathematics

Günter Radden
Cognitive Grammar, metaphor, metonymy, linguistic motivation

Eleanor Rosch
Basic level categories, categorisation, Prototype Theory

Dominiek Sandra
Cognitive lexical semantics, psycholinguistics

Chris Sinha
Cognitive development, the extended mind, distributed spatial semantics, language and intersubjectivity, the evolution of language and cognition

Eve Sweetser
Blending Theory, conditional constructions, discourse analysis, metaphor, modality, Mental Spaces Theory, applications of cognitive semantics to semantic change and meaning-construction

Leonard Talmy
Attention, Conceptual System Structuring Approach, fictive motion, force-dynamics, linguistic evolution, spatial representation in language, sign language

Michael Tomasello
Cognitive development, evolutionary psychology, first language acquisition, language evolution and development

Elizabeth Closs Traugott
Grammaticalisation, Invited Inferencing Theory,
semantic change

Mark Turner
Blending Theory, cognitive poetics, Conceptual
Metaphor Theory, metaphor, application of cognitive
semantics to social science

Andrea Tyler
Application of cognitive linguistics to language
pedagogy, prepositions, Principled Polysemy

Claude Vandeloise
Cognitive lexical semantics, prepositions

Jörg Zinken
Cultural linguistics, discourse analysis, metaphor

Jordan Zlatev
Cognitive lexical semantics, embodied cognition,
mimesis, spatial semantics